International Insolvency and Finance Law

Focusing on the Global Financial Crisis and the Covid-19 crisis, this book examines the discourse on risk and uncertainty in the markets through the lens of financial crises. Such crises represent a failure of the law to regulate and constitute the basis through which a new theory of legal constants can be introduced in comparative law.

Crises impose a dramatic reformulation of the law and new out-of-law instances are appearing beyond a paternalistic approach of direct state regulation, a trend confirmed by the Covid-19 pandemic. Restructuring procedures are playing a vital role in businesses' survival, and new out-of-law mechanisms such as moratorium agreements and private workouts have become essential to preserve businesses. It is clear the role of the law has completely changed, and this book argues that constants outside of the law are new ways to promote an "uncodified-codification" of the law.

The case for uncodified uncertainty in the Covid-19 crisis is a primary example of how no codification process can ignore the importance of out-of-law instances in the act of making law. This book explores how this approach influences the harmonisation process of international economic law between national insolvency regimes and international agreed frameworks, demonstrating the role of comparative law in formulating legal constants using Covid-19 and the complexity of modern financial markets as the criterion to introduce the reader to this new theory, which claims a new role for comparative law in policymaking processes within the framework of international economic law.

Daniele D'Alvia is a Teaching Fellow in Banking and Finance Law at CCLS – Queen Mary University of London, UK, an Associate Research Fellow at IALS, and the Module Convener of Comparative Law at Birkbeck College, University of London, UK. He was the module convener of International Finance and Company Law at the University of Hertfordshire, UK, and a visiting scholar and researcher in global financial markets at the Commercial Law Centre at Harris Manchester College University of Oxford, the International Chamber of Commerce, and the Max Planck Institute for Comparative and International Private Law.

Insights on International Economic Law
Series Editor: David Collins, Professor of International Economic Law at City, University of London.

International Economic Law is among the fastest growing and vibrant fields of international law, responding to the escalating tensions in global trade and investment which take on not only economic and legal but also social and geopolitical dimensions. In many respects the issues of International Economic Law are among the most important of our times, as captured for example in the ongoing fascination with the trade aspects of Brexit, the US-China trade war, security-related fears of foreign investment in critical infrastructure projects and the controversial elements of China's economic expansion into the developing world. The Routledge Insights on International Economic Law series is an important conduit for the dissemination of crucial, socially valuable research, encompassing peer reviewed short-form style books which examine emerging hot topics in international economic law which have reached a pivotal stage of importance.

The Development Dimension: Special and Differential Treatment in Trade
James Bacchus and Inu Manak

International Insolvency and Finance Law: Legal Constants in Times of Crisis
Daniele D'Alvia

https://www.routledge.com/law/series/IIEL

International Insolvency and Finance Law

Legal Constants in Times of Crisis

Daniele D'Alvia

Routledge
Taylor & Francis Group

LONDON AND NEW YORK

First published 2022
by Routledge
2 Park Square, Milton Park, Abingdon, Oxon OX14 4RN

and by Routledge
605 Third Avenue, New York, NY 10158

Routledge is an imprint of the Taylor & Francis Group, an informa business

© 2022 Daniele D'Alvia

British Library Cataloguing-in-Publication Data
A catalogue record for this book is available from the British Library

Library of Congress Cataloging-in-Publication Data
A catalog record has been requested for this book

ISBN: 978-1-032-10792-9 (hbk)
ISBN: 978-1-032-24379-5 (pbk)
ISBN: 978-1-003-27832-0 (ebk)

DOI: 10.4324/9781003278320

Typeset in Times New Roman
by Deanta Global Publishing Services, Chennai, India

We must undergo a hard winter training
and not rush into things for which we haven't prepared.

—Epictetus, Discourses, 1.2.32

To Radomira, my partner, who in the face of human calamities and difficulties has re-evocated in me the importance of appreciating simple things of life without taking care or being worried about our "metallic substances".

D.

Contents

Acknowledgements   ix
List of Abbreviations   x

Introduction   1

1   The Times of Crisis between Insolvency and Financial Law   9

    1.1 The Legal Theory of Finance 9
    1.2 The Global Financial Crisis (2007–2010) 15
          1.2.1 Risk and Uncertainty 19
          1.2.2 The Role of the Law in Financial Crisis 19
          1.2.3 The 2020 Unfolding Crisis: Covid-19 21
    1.3 The Evolution of Corporate Insolvency Law Regimes 24
          1.3.1 The Private and Public Divide in Insolvency Law 26
          1.3.2 Contractarian and Out-of-Law Approaches 29
    *1.4 Comparative Law as a Policymaking Instrument of
          "Out-of-Law" Meanings 34*
    1.5 Conclusions 35

2   Legal Constants, and the Constant Outside of the Law   38

    2.1 Theories of Comparative Law: The Law as "Input" 38
          2.1.1 The Functions and Aims of Comparative Law 40
          *2.1.2 Comparative Law as a Tool for Studying (Legal)
                  Meanings 41*
    2.2 Legal Constant(s) 41
          *2.2.1 The Constant(s) Outside of the Law and Legal
                  Constant(s) 42*
          *2.2.2 The Development of Legal Constants in Commercial
                  Law 44*

2.3 The Uncodified-Codification of the Law 46
2.3.1 The Uncodified Law and Crisis 47
2.4 Conclusions 47

3   The Un(codified) Financial Systems in Times of Crisis   50

3.1 The Ontology of Risk 50
3.1.1 The Epistemology of Risk 53
3.2 The Ontology of Uncertainty 54
3.2.1 The Role of Uncertainty 55
3.3 The Structures of Markets 55
3.3.1 The Financial Systems and Complexity 58
3.3.2 Competition and Financial Innovation 59
3.4 The New Legal Theory of Finance 59
3.4.1 The Un(codified) Role of Uncertainty 60
3.5 Conclusions 61

4   Cross-Border Insolvency Law: Venturing Beyond Structural Crisis   63

4.1 International Insolvency Law 63
4.1.1 The Role of Contract Law versus Statute Law 64
4.2 The Global Legal Indicators 67
*4.2.1 The UNCITRAL Legislative Guide on Insolvency
Law 69*
*4.2.2 The World Bank Principles for Effective Insolvency and
Creditor/Debtor Regimes 71*
*4.2.3 The EBRD Core Principles of an Effective Insolvency
System 72*
4.3 The New Financial Architecture 73
4.3.1 Macro- versus Micro-Legislations 74
4.4 Conclusions 77

Conclusions   79
Index   85

Acknowledgements

Market auto-regeneration processes or autopoiesis in times of crises are important. This is because, beyond every structural financial turmoil and human catastrophe, we can still find or seek the light if we start learning how to re-evaluate uncertainty in positive and metaphysical terms.

The ideas I have shared and written in this short book are mainly a recollection of thoughts I first had when I was 27 years old, and that I have later developed in research papers and books. It is generally said that people under 30 years old tend to have "big ideas". I do not know about the consistency or truthfulness of such a statement because as much as I love my work, I also hate it in the same measure. Writing is exposing oneself to public opinion, and sometimes the same activity of writing becomes a challenging task even more during a pandemic and in times of crisis. The appearance of Covid-19 in 2020 has irremediably changed the world but still has not been able to change ourselves. Indeed, I am grateful to many of my students to whom I had been privileged to teach both at Birkbeck College and Queen Mary University of London during these years in London. Students have been a living and inspiring source of motivation for my studies and even more during a pandemic.

Specifically, the inspiration for writing about international insolvency law has come from my involvement as a consultant at the EBRD between 2020 and 2021 where I had the opportunity to work on the insolvency law assessment of 38 countries of operation. I am thankful to my colleagues Prof. Rodrigo Olivares-Caminal and Prof. John Taylor, who are also colleagues of mine at Queen Mary University of London, and the Legal Transition Team Programme's Financial Law Unit at the EBRD: Catherine Bridge Zoller (Senior Counsel) and Hanna Volchak (Associate). I am also particularly grateful to three other special colleagues with whom I had the pleasure to work at the EBRD: Natalia Pagkou, Guido Demarco, and Nino Goglidze.

List of Abbreviations

BRRD	Bank Recovery and Resolution Directive 2014/59/EU establishing a framework for the recovery and resolution of credit institutions and investment firms
CAC	Collective action clause
DSSI	Debt service suspension initiative
EBRD	European Bank for Reconstruction and Development
ESG	Environmental, social, and corporate governance
Fed	Federal Reserve System
Fintech	Financial technology
GDP	Gross Domestic Product
GFC	Global Financial Crisis
ICMA	International Capital Market Association
IMF	International Monetary Fund
INSOL International	International Association of Restructuring, Insolvency and Bankruptcy Professionals
IPO	Initial public offering
ISDA	International Swaps and Derivatives Association
LFT	Legal theory of finance
LOLR	Lender of Last Resort
Recast Insolvency Regulation	Regulation 2015/848/EU on insolvency proceedings (recast)
Restructuring Directive	Directive 2019/1023/EU on preventive restructuring frameworks, discharge of debt and disqualifications, and measures to increase the efficiency of procedure concerning restructuring, insolvency, and discharged debt, amending Directive (EU) 2017/1132
SME	Small-medium enterprise
UNCITRAL	United Nations Commission on International Trade Law
UNIDROIT	International Institute for the Unification of Private Law
WBG	World Bank Group

Introduction

The beginning of 2020 was impacted by an unanticipated event that will have profound consequences for the decade to come. On 25 May 2020, George Floyd, a black man who was killed by a white police officer in Minneapolis in the United States, sparked protest marches in countries around the world, including the UK. Many of the protesters marched as part of the Black Lives Matter movement – a de-centralised global network that campaigns for justice, equality, and an end to racism. In the UK, several statutes were pulled down or had words of protest written on them. These statutes were generally historical figures with links to the slave trade, for instance, the statute of Edward Colston in Bristol. While on the streets there are chants of "Stop Killing Black People!" and "No justice, no peace!", behind a computer, one of the millions of new day traders buys a stock because the chart is quickly moving higher.[1]

The stock market was shaken in March 2020 at the outset of the Covid-19 outbreak, but then something happened. Although hundreds of thousands of lives were lost, millions of people were laid off and businesses shuttered, and the outgoing president of the United States of America was refusing to accept the outcome of the 2020 election, for weeks and months, the stock market soared. Think of special purpose acquisition companies, which by the end of 2020 raised almost $83 billion in initial public offering (IPO) proceeds, and just in the first quarter of 2021, almost $98 billion. There is an explanation for this. First, the Federal Reserve took extraordinary measures to support financial markets and promote economic stability.[2] The Federal Reserve tried to make it cheap for all kinds of entities to get loans while hoping public health officials could get the virus under

---

1 Chris Brown wrote this in a letter to investors in June 2020 (Chris Brown is the founder and managing member of the Ohio-based hedge fund Aristides Capital), available at https://assets.empiref inancialresearch.com/uploads/2020/06/Aristides-Fund-letter-6-3-20.pdf, accessed on 13 July 2021.
2 Federal Reserve, "Federal Reserve announces extensive new measures to support the economy" (23 March 2020) Press Release, available at www.federalreserve.gov/newsevents/pressreleases/monetary20200323b.htm, accessed on 17 July 2021. Historically, the Federal Reserve approach to stabilise the economy was largely limited to setting short-term interest rates. For instance, during the Great Recession, short-term rates went to zero and the economy was still depressed. That led the Federal Reserve to undertake multiple rounds of what is confusingly come to be known as "quan-

DOI: 10.4324/9781003278320-1

control and Congress could act to provide the kinds of economic support that only it could offer. However, interest rates were already low at the start of the coronavirus crisis: the Fed cut rates on 3 March[3] and then again, all the way down to zero on 15 March.[4] This move represented the clearest sign yet that the Fed considered the coronavirus outbreak a severe economic risk that could slow the economy and possibly cause a large recession. Then it rapidly announced a plan for $700 billion in quantitative easing. Second, Congress also did its part, pumping trillions of dollars into the economy across multiple relief bills. It seems that giving people money is good for markets, too. And with bond yields so low, investors did not really have a more lucrative place to put their money, so they decided to invest in stocks. In other words, the stock market is not representative of the whole economy, and the stock market was just fine. Hence, the next question should be: should the system work on those assumptions? Essentially, in traditional monetary policy, short-term interest rates are the lever that moves the whole economy? It seems that rates on long-term government bonds go down when short-term rates go down, and rates on corporate debt go down when rates on government debt go down. Essentially, although short-term rates are not in themselves so important, the profit-seeking traders ensure that the impact spreads throughout the economy. In other words, speculation makes financial markets move, and the essence of every speculator is a willingness to face uncertainty (see Chapter 3). This work would like to claim that, as opposed to Pistor's view, in the face of a liquidity shortage, uncertainty is a driving force of market economies and is a source of profit.

It is undeniable that the pandemic known as Covid-19 is an unprecedented crisis that has stopped the world economy at various times of the year since its appearance in March 2020. Covid-19 has created an economic as well as a human calamity that is measured in a global sea of debt that will take at least a decade to reduce to normal levels. According to Kristalina Georgieva (managing director of the International Monetary Fund [IMF]), who in late 2020 used the term "economic calamity", we have seen global fiscal actions of $12trn through which central banks have expanded balance sheets by $7.5trn. The IMF is expecting 2021 debt levels to go up significantly to around 125% of gross domestic product (GDP) in advanced economies, 65% in emerging markets, and 50% in low-income industries. The answers at regional and international levels have been determined by new injections of "money" into the system. For instance, the European Union has a programme called Next Generation EU that is tiding over the next few years to the tune of more than $876bn in the form of grants and loans. However, the

---

titative easing", which means the Fed announces it is going to buy such-and-such billion dollars' worth of longer-term bonds and then goes out and does that.
3   Federal Reserve, "Federal Reserve issues FOMC statement" (3 March 2020) Press Release, available at www.federalreserve.gov/newsevents/pressreleases/monetary20200303a.htm, accessed on 3 July 2021.
4   Ibid.

eurozone's latest economic growth figures are little better than expected.[5] While US and Chinese economies are both bigger than their 2019 peaks, the eurozone is 3% off that achievement.

From a regulatory perspective, as opposed to previous recent economic crises, namely the 2007–2010 Global Financial Crisis (GFC) and the 2010–2018 sovereign debt crisis in the eurozone, a recent study has shown[6] how the new unfolding crisis of Covid-19 is mild in respect of the stability of the EU financial system. This is because the pandemic is an exogenous factor rather than an internal cause of failure of the financial system, and the financial regulatory framework had become much more robust in the meantime, although financial regulation is irremediably destined to fail in its aim to regulate uncertainty and operational risks (see Chapters 1 and 3).

Nonetheless, it is undeniable that Covid-19 has reshaped consumer behaviour and the way we do business across the world. Much of the economic activity of most countries has been hindered and one of the first effects of the pandemic was a sharp decline in most financial markets, with the notable exception of less liquid assets, such as alternative assets. Among them, we find private debt instruments. The growth of private debt is not a new phenomenon, and it arose out of the 2007 financial crisis, at a time when governments consolidated the regulation of international banking. Think of the Basel III agreements published in December 2010.

Essentially, the primordial idea was to connect the crisis to the growth of excessive bank financing. Regulators concluded that restrictions on certain types of financing were the way to limit systemic risk. From that moment on, banks have been required to keep more cash in reserve for lending to businesses, rather than loans to governments. This means that some businesses have less access to credit or no access at all. Even if your company has positive earnings before interest, taxes, depreciation, and amortisation, this does not guarantee that the business can be accreditable to receive financing from banks. This has opened up a definite opportunity for investors, both institutional and private, to fill the vacuum. Private debt instruments might have some advantages for the portfolio of investors, namely higher yield and the absence of a direct connection to market volatility. Investing in private debt means scarifying liquidity for a higher return and capital stability.

This, in turn, has given rise to the acknowledgement that the level of private debt cannot be ignored, and it is destined to play a central role in contemporary financial markets both in terms of access to finance and as a remarkable sign of

---

5 Philip Blenkinsop, Balazs Koranyi, "Euro zone growth rebounds, inflation tops ECB target" (30 July 2021) Reuters, available at www.reuters.com/world/europe/euro-zone-rebounds-strongly -inflation-above-ecb-target-2021-07-30/, accessed on 10 August 2021.
6 Christos V. Gortsos, Wolf-Georg Ringe, *Financial Stability amidst the Pandemic Crisis: On Top of the Wave* (European Banking Institute 2021).

the intrinsic nature of financial systems to fail by virtue of systemic risk and moral hazard.

The American philanthropist Richard Vague[7] has examined all major economic crises since 1850 and concluded that two key signs of an imminent crisis are private debt exceeding 1.5 times GDP, and the ratio rising by 17 percentage points or more over five years. For instance, in the UK, private debt rose from 135% of GDP in 2000 to 180% when the GFC began in August 2007 – a 45% rise in less than eight years. In the same periods, the United States followed a similar pattern with a 35% figure. Those rates of change were unsustainable, and while in the 1980s and 1990s policymakers believed that controlling the money supply was the key to lower inflation and faster growth, in the past two decades, central banks have been given greater responsibility for managing the economy and securing financial stability. After the GFC, and again after the unfolding crisis generated by the pandemic in 2020, governments rediscovered the power of fiscal policy. Central banks have played a central role in enabling this rise in public spending while tax revenues are down by buying up government debt in record amounts through quantitative easing. As a result, global long-term interest rates fell to historical lows in 2008 and have continued falling since. The huge growth in central banks' balance sheets since 2008 is the result of such activity, namely, to buy government debt and also some private debt so that financial systems can absorb vast amounts of new borrowing. After more than a decade of this extreme monetary relaxation, inflation has hit the markets once again as was acknowledged in August 2021 at Jackson Hole, Wyoming, for the annual gathering of the world's central bankers trying to "save the world". Here, the Federal Reserve Chairman, Jerome Powell, confirmed the decision to taper off the Federal Reserve's $120 billion in monthly asset purchases without the need for increasing interest rates from their near-zero levels. Indeed, in the last quarter of 2021, US inflation was above 5% and since then the Federal Reserve has been under particular pressure to raise interest rates or help curb inflation. While the world is focused on "leaning-against-the-wind", environmentalists argue that low interest rates are essential in order to borrow cheaply to fund massive carbon-reduction investments.

Covid-19 is difficult to overcome, and it might become a permanent endemic feature of our economies (Chapter 3). Nonetheless, countries are likely to recover at different speeds, although the lack of access to vaccines in emerging economies will lead to new inequalities. This is exacerbated by the fact that, according to modern monetary theory, nothing is wrong with governments continually borrowing heavily at low interest rates. As Covid-19 spreads, central bankers are demanding a bigger fiscal response to spread the burden of sparking a recovery. This is because low interest rates are under fire for exacerbating inequality, as the rich countries tend to gain more from swollen asset prices than the rest do from higher output and employment.

---

7 Richard Vague, *A Brief History of Doom: Two Hundred Years of Financial Crisis* (University of Pennsylvania Press 2019).

For those reasons, the recovery of every country depends on several factors, including the effectiveness of recovery policies and how they deal with high sovereign debts.

However, financial markets might find their own solutions to a crisis through their own market operators: private equity funds. Despite Covid-inflicted disruptions, the private equity industry has evolved significantly during the last few decades, and the industry attests to the fact that the days when private equity investments were basically meant to keep companies afloat are long gone. When the private equity industry started two decades ago, the traditional model was of private equity firms buying into undervalued companies, building them up and then exiting. While private equity firms are not ready to entirely discard this model, a shift towards the principles of sustainability guided by environmental, social, and corporate governance (ESG) is emerging. This is a powerful force for sustainable economic development. Private equity investors are looking for a longer-term perspective beyond the five-year investment horizon, and they tend to invest in high growth companies in sectors like technology, media and telecom, medical infrastructures, renewable energies, and so on. The industry is looking to invest particularly in emerging markets and developing nations such as Asia, South America, Latin America, and Africa. Indeed, in developing countries, the private sector is the engine of economic growth, job creation, and poverty alleviation, and private equity firms have amassed substantial experience investing in private companies. This is where the main challenge rests for developing countries, as Covid-19 has caused devastating damage to the private sector.

However, emerging markets must undertake structural adjustments to create an environment that is conducive to growing the pie of private equity investments. This includes increased transparency, better governance, and supportive regulatory environments. Indeed, the interest of private actors, such as private equity firms, in investing in emerging economies also depends on their level of modernisation of the law, especially in strategic commercial law areas such as corporate insolvency law. For instance, access to new financing for the corporate restructuring of distressed businesses is essential, as well as dynamic and flexible corporate insolvency frameworks that recognise a new emerging "rescue culture" as well as the importance of preventive restructuring (see Chapters 1 and 4).

This work would like to highlight how within complex financial markets, the role of uncertainty is maximised. In light of this, uncertainty is not the trigger for crisis because it underpins money creation processes. Based on this assumption, this work claims that the role of the law has been irremediably changed. *Contra* Pistor, the codification process of the law is no longer based on the assumption that the law is an "input" but rather an "output". For example, to modernise the insolvency law framework of a developing country, we no longer need a state law inspired by the elected members of parliament. The modernisation of the law, today, is a process that necessarily starts from the acknowledgement of common non-legal meanings or the interpretation of legal principles that can inspire the enactment of hard laws. For example, we have just mentioned the new role of sustainability, both with reference to sovereign debt and private investments.

Sustainability is a common word that has a shared common meaning, and it is the word or better password of the new financial architecture of capital markets. Indeed, sustainability is a direct instance and one of the most prominent examples of what I define as legal constant(s) in comparative law theory (see Chapter 2). Essentially, a constant is found within non-legal words or non-legal meanings that are derived from the activity of interpretation. Those non-legal meanings or non-legal words are shared by several legal cultures within different countries and populations. This is because the non-legal nature of a constant is more easily shared and recognised by many. A constant is often neutral, beyond the political considerations that usually inform policy decisions. Those common meanings are then discussed first and foremost at the international level, usually by non-state organisations (see Chapters, 1, 2, and 4). Subsequently, it is again the law as "output" that confers a legal and binding effect to those common meanings or constants that they eventually become "legal", such as when the entire national corporate insolvency law framework of a country is reformed following the advice of insolvency law assessments conducted by multilateral banking institutions such as the European Bank for Reconstruction and Development (EBRD). Other times, even the simple inclusion of those constants in soft law instruments is able to alter hard law instances of national legal provisions such as in the case of the International Swaps and Derivatives Association (ISDA) Common Domain Model that is a blueprint for how derivatives are traded. This also gives comparative law a new, incredible importance in the shaping of the future of financial markets and markets' economies. Indeed, it is this new tendency to find out the most compatible constant that is inducing countries to seek further cooperation at the international level in order to establish the non-legal meanings that hard law instances will be ready to follow in each country. Hence, implementation phases at the national level are semantically transformed into a new law paradigm that is focused on translating a non-legal meaning into a hard law meaning. This new theory of comparative law deeply informs this book, and I would like it to give rise to further discussions on the new emerging instances of the law as "output" rather than "input" (see Chapters 1, 2, and 4).

In addition to those theoretical aspects that the book aims to cover for the first time in comparative law, this work is focused on financial markets, and it outlines the subtle and intimate connections that exist between two key areas of the law, namely insolvency law and finance law. This is because, in the new "rescue culture" of insolvency law frameworks, there is no viable saving of businesses without appropriate financing measures and protections for secured creditors. It seems that today, access to finance means access to being part of an international entourage of non-state actors where cooperation mechanisms and soft law instruments are agreed upon and shared across multiple different countries and regions of the world. This new role of the law also implies a new role of comparative law – as we have outlined before – that becomes a new policy instrument. In the end, the role of a central planner in the new financial architecture of capital markets is absent (see Chapters 1, 2, and 4), and hard law frameworks at national level start to be assessed on their efficiency rather than quality. The unit measure of such efficiency is always more often provided by comparative law reports or assessments promoted by non-state organisations and measured through indicators that are deputed to evaluate the growth of a country as well as its national legislative framework against agreed benchmarks – often established at international level (see Chapters 1 and 4). For these reasons, the private and public divide that originally characterised the birth of the modern state after the French Revolution has been dramatically reformed. There is no more private and no more public, but a hybrid of public and private, as are the areas of the law of international finance and insolvency.

In the face of this new paradigm of contemporary financial markets based on market practices and agreed principles, we face new threats that cut across climate change, environmental pollution, bad governance, corruption, and technology failure, to name a few. In Africa, for instance, climate change is a major threat to human health and safety. It is not surprising that the first major assessment in August 2021 from the UN-backed Intergovernmental Panel on Climate Change sees no end to rising temperatures before 2050. Like the last two in 2014 and 2018, this report confirms that to achieve the goal of 2015's Paris Agreement, global emissions need to peak by around 2025 and then plunge rapidly towards zero. Catastrophes are befalling the atmosphere, the oceans, the ice packs, and the forests, and nearly all of this can be attributed to human influence; without drastic moves by the planet's leaders to eliminate greenhouse gas pollution, things are going to get a lot worse, and quite soon. The report is not a binding legal instrument; instead, it represents the emergence of the soft law and cooperation agreements that we introduced a few lines above. The report suggests changes in different sectors like electricity, construction, and transport, from which many of the emissions come. Those measures include, *inter alia*, a ban on new fossil fuel infrastructure, radical improvements in the energy efficiency of buildings, and the replacement of coal plants with renewable sources of energy. The central question here is: how to finance this rapid shift? This entails mobilising investment in renewable energy, doing huge amounts of retrofitting buildings for energy efficiency, and so on. It is a question that can entail dealing with global inequalities in emissions, but the main issue is how to mobilise those funds. The neoliberal consensus is to favour private finance. This once again can confirm how access to finance depends on liberal markets, but those markets have to compete with each other to get the right amount of capital. Again, uncertainty is key to promoting those virtuous competition mechanisms, because without uncertainty there is no profit, and without the possibility of seeking profit, there would not be any competition or financial innovation. For these reasons, this book aims to theorise financial markets as financial systems, under a new interpretation of Luhmann's system theory, where markets can be interpreted as systems composed of four main structures: risk, uncertainty, competition, and financial innovation (see Chapters 1 and 3).

In the end, beyond the financial crises that will always, undeniably, characterise capitalist systems, new, emerging crises may shape the world, such as the humanitarian crisis triggered by developments in Afghanistan with the Taliban government or the environmental crisis from which our planet seems unable to escape, or even an important cyber-attack on a massive scale or a simple technology failure that might affect the new structures of de-centralised finance. Ironically the same democratisation of financial markets through alternative forms of private money such as Bitcoin, Stablecoin, and so on might find its intrinsic form of collapse deriving from a possible failure of its most important structure: the blockchain technology. These crises are necessarily looking for new solutions that are always more often based on non-legal words or non-legal meanings. "Sustainability", "environment", "green", "diversity", and "network": these are just some of the many non-legal words or better in a digitalised financial ecosystem, passwords that today inform hard law instances and are capable of marginalising the law in its secular vision as the "input" of the state and an obsolete and inappropriate Westphalian model of the law. In a digital era, passwords or constants outside of the law are the keys to the future rather than legal definitions.

1 The Times of Crisis between Insolvency and Financial Law

1.1 The Legal Theory of Finance

In 2013, Katharina Pistor wrote a working paper at Columbia Law School titled "A Legal Theory of Finance".[1] In it, Pistor claims that finance is legally constructed; this means that finance does not stand outside the law. For example, Pistor makes the case that financial assets are disciplined by legal rules and regulators. Although this can vary from jurisdiction to jurisdiction, the legal enforcement of financial commitments is present in every jurisdiction and can influence the scope of the entire financial system. In other words, without legal enforcement, contractual promises cannot be honoured, and the capital outflows or inflows between jurisdictions cannot be effective. For this reason, market participants often design financial instruments that are not in conflict with the existing rules in different jurisdictions. It means that contract law plays a major role in contemporary financial markets, and contractual rules are able to provide financial operators as well as the financial industry with new contractual devices, which – according to Pistor – in turn, seek legal vindication.

In claiming legal vindication, financial operators can try to mitigate uncertainty and prevent liquidity volatility. According to Pistor, liquidity is not a free asset, and when the future shows a liquidity scarcity, the refinance of financial commitments becomes more challenging. This is because every financial system is inherently unstable, and the exercise of discretionary power to enforce legal commitments can bring about a new theory of political economy of finance.

Pistor takes into account a conception of liquidity borrowed from Bernanke.[2] From this perspective, liquidity is connected to the ability to sell any asset for other assets or cash at will. For instance, in a business reorganisation procedure we might think of carve-out mergers and acquisitions transactions and the dismissal of business' going concern (*i.e.* the selling of an asset for cash), and in respect of financial markets, we can imagine any secondary market where the

---

1 Katharina Pistor, "A legal theory of finance" (2013) Paper Number 13-348 Columbia Law School – Public & Legal Theory Working Paper Group 13.
2 Ben Bernanke, "The great moderation" (20 February 2004) Federal Reserve, available at www.federalreserve.gov/boarddocs/speeches/2004/20040220/defaul.htm, accessed on 10 December 2021.

DOI: 10.4324/9781003278320-2

investor is selling financial instruments, being they derivatives, bonds, or stocks, to second-hand investors. In sovereign debt restructuring practices: an exchange offer or debt-for-debt swap or through the use of an internal collective action mechanism[3] (if included in the debt instrument).

To this end, Pistor defines liquidity shortage, namely the impossibility of finding second-hand investors willing to buy financial assets, as one of the main triggers of a financial crisis. Specifically, she claims that uncertainty, rather than underpinning money creation processes, undermines the possibility of obtaining new financing and, therefore, it qualifies liquidity shortage in terms of crisis. Consequently, if financial assets are legally constructed, the law directly contributes to finance's instability. The main example that is brought to the attention of the reader is the case of sovereign debt. The law of the issuer, namely the national law of the country that is borrowing money from investors through a Eurobond, matters, because at the apex, the law is much more flexible in comparison with the periphery (the contractual terms and conditions of a bond prospectus or the offering memorandum or circular). Indeed, at the apex, the law is more elastic because the survival of the entire system is at stake, and the discretionary power can be limited to save the system. On the other hand, at the periphery, the law is less elastic, and default can result in an involuntary exit. Furthermore, if we agree with this vision, we must consequently admit that the survival of the system is determined at its apex.

Specifically, states or financial intermediaries are in greater proximity to the apex. Hence, they are also more likely to benefit from a relaxation of the rules or a suspension of the full force of the law. A direct example can be seen in sovereign debt contracts whose enforceability is doubtful, or elastic. States' assets cannot be seized and liquidated, and only assets located overseas can be frozen (if ever). In other words, a state cannot be subject to liquidation as happens in the case of private distressed companies that might be liquidated if they do not find a viable alternative to restructure their finances. Furthermore, sovereign governments that owe debt to many foreign creditors can choose which creditors to favour when making payments by implementing a *de facto* seniority structure of sovereign debt.[4] Essentially, the state issuing sovereign debt can "escape" legal obligation by changing the law or altering the order of priority of payments. However, finan-

---

3 Historically, collective action clauses (CACs) derive from the failure of the IMF's proposal for a Sovereign Debt Restructuring Mechanism (SDRM), perhaps the best-known attempt to create a multilateral sovereign debt framework in the early 2000s. The private creditor community actively lobbied creditor-hosting governments and debtor states against the SDRM by presenting an alternative, more market-friendly approach to debt restructuring: CACs. CACs benefit private creditors by allowing them to remain in control of their loans to debtors during crises. In contrast, a multilateral sovereign debt framework would be capable of overriding debt financing contracts, imposing a stay on creditor litigation, and brokering debt restructuring under the auspices of a defined framework, to the detriment of private creditors.

4 Matthias Schlegl, Christoph Trebesch, Mark L. J. Wright, "The seniority structure of sovereign debt" (May 2019) Research Division Federal Reserve Bank of Minneapolis – Working Paper 759, 1.

ciers have been able to sue their own sovereigns for default. The Brady Plan of the 1980s was the turning point for sovereign debt litigation;[5] today's investors in sovereign debt markets differ from a handful of major syndicated commercial banks prior to the Brady Plan. The growth of secondary sovereign bond markets and the transferability of bonds have opened up access to a wide range of new investors, including professional sovereign debt litigants. These are distressed debt funds that have taken advantage of a business opportunity presented by the secondary market in the absence of a sovereign bankruptcy regime to operate a business model based on sovereign litigation. They have been labelled "vulture funds" as they acquire defaulted (or nearly defaulted) sovereign debt at a significant discount from their issue price on the secondary market, with a premeditated view to hold out[6] from a restructuring and to litigate for the debt's full face value with interest and delay penalties, and subsequently pursuing the debtor country's assets to realise the full value of the claim.[7] They sue sovereigns in multiple jurisdictions in order to seize sovereign assets to satisfy their court judgements.

Under the threat of potential litigation, states try to pay the majority of debt the majority of the time in the hope that this can more easily enable them to access further financing through capital markets and official sector intervention. On the other hand, the litigation risk has exponentially escalated due to the fact that sovereigns frequently issue debt to foreign investors. The latter have brought arbitration proceedings against the state once it defaults on its external debt.

Arbitration is also the field that allows us to make some preliminary reflections on soft law. Historically, the contractual right to choose soft law as the governing law has been narrowly restricted to arbitration. For instance, the Uniform Commercial Code provides the closest US non-arbitration precedent, allowing parties to vary their provisions by choosing soft law promulgated by intergovernmental authorities, such as the United Nations Commission on International Trade Law (UNCITRAL) or the International Institute for the Unification of Private Law (UNIDROIT), or to trade codes such as the Uniform Customs and Practice for Documentary Credits. The Hague Principles on Choice of Law in International Commercial Contracts also favour the right to parties to choose "rules of soft law" that "are generally accepted on an international, supranational or regional level as a neutral and balanced set of rules". It seems that international commercial,

---

5 The Brady Plan involved exchanging outstanding commercial bank loans for bonds in order to relieve the emerging market debt crisis of the late 1980s and early 1990s.

6 Holdout litigation has proliferated since courts have explicitly upheld the vulture funds' business model of the late 1990s. In *Elliot Associates v Republic of Peru* (1998), the US Court of Appeals dismissed Peru's champerty defence on the grounds that Elliot's principal intent was to be paid in full and that Elliot's litigation was incidental and contingent on Peru's non-performance of obligations under the contract. Champerty prohibited the purchase of debt with the intent and for the purpose of bringing a lawsuit. The court rejected the champerty defence even though it was clear that at the time of buying Peru's debt, Elliot, a vulture fund, would have known that Peru would not be able to pay in full. Vulture funds then lobbied in NY legislature in 2004 to amend the NY Judiciary Law 489 so as to prevent the defence of champerty from arising for any debt purchases above $500,000.

7 Julian Schumacher and others, "Sovereign defaults in court" (2018) ECB Working Paper 2135, 17.

financial, and other business transactions are increasingly conducted under "soft law" rules, which are non-state rules that may be aspirational or reflect best practices but are not yet legally enforceable. The attraction to soft law is focused on the fact that it does not need governmental validation or consent. Nonetheless, it is undeniable that the law still plays a vital role in shaping the enforcement of legal obligations. The law and the power that is exercised by the state can effectively change the level of enforcement and vindication. By contrast, soft law can be seen as a reliable methodology to provide parties with friendly regulatory frameworks that are seen as a non-mechanical form of regulation. Indeed, parties tend to spontaneously adhere to soft law frameworks rather than hard law, which is often perceived as a sort of external imposition. For this reason, it has sometimes been said that soft law is harder than hard law.[8]

This dynamic evolution of regulatory regimes has contributed to the exponential growth of hybrid models of regulation. For instance, a new hybrid model of the law has consented to the exponential growth of swaps and derivatives contracts. Indeed, the International Swaps and Derivatives Association (ISDA) has played a major role in the rise of derivatives by creating standard contracts and adapting them to different legal systems around the world. In other words, the ISDA was formed to develop templates for derivative instruments that would be enforceable in multiple jurisdictions. This is a direct example of the critical role that the law is playing in shaping the future, and indirectly in allowing private organisations discretionary power to determine market practices. This is, according to Pistor, the establishment of a central planner that can exercise its authority and power in order to influence the legal environment. The central planner can be a public entity such as the state or a private organisation such as the ISDA, whose objective is to ensure that critical pieces of legislation validate the contracts it sponsors.

The same example can be found in sovereign debt, with the International Capital Market Association (ICMA), which, in 2014, published a new standard of the *pari passu* clause for inclusion in the terms and conditions of sovereign debt securities, and an updated version of the aggregated collective action clauses for the terms and conditions of sovereign notes.[9] A very good example of the application of those principles comes from the final restructuring deal that Argentina reached with its foreign bondholders in early August 2020 in the form of a bond exchange offer that was approved overwhelmingly by its foreign bondholders. The tortuous negotiating process lasted several months and came after Argentina had defaulted on its sovereign debt in late May 2020 for the ninth time in its history. On the issue of collective action clauses (CACs), prominent professors around the world wrote open letters to express their strong support for Argentina's

---

8 Francis Snyder, "Soft law and governance: Aspects of the European Union experience" in Luo Haocai (ed) *The European Union Experience* (Peking University Press 2009).

9 International Capital Markets Association, "Standard collective action and pari passu clauses for the terms and conditions of sovereign notes" (2014) available at www.icmagroup.org/Regulatory -Policy-and-Market-Practice/Primary-Markets/primary-market-topics/collective-action-clauses/, accessed on 7 July 2021.

negotiating position.[10] Specifically, those professors claimed that CACs based on aggregated voting across multiple series of bonds should be incorporated in the new bonds, as opposed to CACs that contained a requirement for series-by-series voting (a position that was favoured by certain bondholders). This is because aggregated CACs became the market standard as embodied in the model promulgated in 2014 by the ICMA and earlier-generation CACs based on series-by-series voting essentially only strengthened the hand of potential holdout creditors. Those are standard contractual terms to ensure the legal enforcement of financial obligations.

Pistor points out the critical and central role of law in financial contracting that is reflected in the fact that every financial intermediary who would like to issue a new financial instrument employs lawyers to check its compliance with laws and regulations. This practice also gives rise to so-called regulatory arbitrage, namely a practice through which financial innovation is in Pistor's view made rule-compliant. In other words, for every legal enforcement of obligations, we might find ways to "escape" those obligations.

What really matters is the nature of power that is exercised and the interests that are protected. For any protected interest, many unprotected ones cannot find reasonable satisfaction, such as in the case of foreign investors and the external debt of a sovereign state. In such cases, the law is creating a "global hierarchy of finance" where transactions can take different forms depending on parties and their importance in the financial ecosystem. Law matters for the position of different actors within the hierarchy, and therefore, it is not possible to conceive of "unregulated" financial markets. Indeed, as we said, the increasing role of non-state actors (ISDA, ICMA, etc.) is a direct confirmation – at least in Pistor's eyes – that financial markets are based on a system of law where sometimes private actors or organisations or States (namely, those closest to the apex) are determining the hierarchy of financial market operators as well as informing the legal enforceability of financial instruments. This is the main reason that a legal theory of finance (LTF) can effectively determine a new paradigm of political economy.

This primordial thinking of financial markets provided by Pistor has been further developed in her latest theory, denominated the "Code of Capital",[11] where she argues that capital has been codified for centuries by means of the law. In her view, the "law is code". Hence, codification becomes the main instrument through which power and private interests can be protected and sometimes this even goes against the primary preservation of vulnerable parties, such as indigenous property rights in the era of colonisation.

---

10 Joseph E. Stiglitz, Edmund S. Phelps, Carmen M. Reinhart, "Restructuring Argentina's private debt is essential" (6 May 2020) available at www.project-syndicate.org/commentary/argentina-sovereign-debt-restructuring-private-creditors-by-joseph-e-stiglitz-et-al-2020-05, accessed on 13 June 2021.

11 Katharina Pistor, *The Code of Capital: How Law Creates Wealth and Inequality* (1st edn, Princeton University Press 2019).

By contrast, this book would like to focus on a new role that comparative law can play in financial crisis, and in the unfolding one triggered by Covid-19, based on what I define as the "uncodified" process of the law. Indeed, the Covid-19 pandemic has imposed a dramatic reformulation of the rule of law, giving way to a more flexible and dynamic form of regulation where traditional instances of statute law are unable to provide answers to new legal issues.

It seems that Pistor's theory can be turned on its head. In other words, today, the law is "dead", and it is not the starting point of our discourse. In a Covid-19 scenario and even before, in the period of the Global Financial Crisis, we are, and we were, all out-of-the-law. Hence, the need to re-discover constant(s) outside of the law: essentially, commercial common concepts or common meanings that are not necessarily "legal" but are shared by many legal systems. In other words, they are uncodified shared/common meanings to be found many times in soft law or self-regulation instruments, namely non-binding legal instruments. Once they are identified, they are used to promote the creation of harmonisation processes through which the law can subsequently identify a common legal meaning to be codified in domestic legislation. This is the phenomenon that I define as the "uncodified-codification" of the law (see Chapters 2 and 4 to have a practical instance of this phenomenon). It means that any codification process must necessarily start from an uncodified and out-of-law identification of (legal) meaning(s).

Essentially, as opposed to Pistor, the law is not the input to codify the capital or to construe financial assets, but rather the output that is the result of an identification and recognition of constant meaning(s) outside of the law. This is also a new way to look at comparative law; not as a science to compare different legal systems, or in Pistor's terms, different codifications, in order to highlight commonalities and differences, and to identify a global code by virtue of "exporting the law". This is still a simplistic comparison of laws similar to Sacco, or Watson with his "legal transplants" (see Chapter 2). It is descriptive rather than dynamic. By contrast, comparative law must be re-invented and re-interpreted to study different meanings that are mainly to be found outside of the law. This is what I define as (legal) constants. Basically, in mathematical terms, it is a negative expression where the inputs, the constant(s) are always outside of the law and only become legal once they are identified and recognised throughout the legal systems. This thinking paves the way to explore the "uncodified-codification" of the law in depth and it connects, for instance, those concepts that are imposed by new market realities to the new insolvency law frameworks that are not by chance focused on business restructuring and out-of-court proceedings. Law is no more at the centre of the system. The system is de-centralised, as de-centralised is the new emerging form of finance through Bitcoin, cryptocurrencies, de-centralised exchanges by virtue of smart contracts, and Special Purpose Acquisition Companies that together are able to disrupt the common wisdom of investing and financing.[12] To this end, even

---

12 Daniele D'Alvia, "SPACs: Why investors fell in love with these stock market vehicles – and how the bubble burst" (22 June 2021) The Conversation, available at https://theconversation.com/spacs

direct listings are no longer directed by underwriters or financial intermediaries, basically, the actors that Pistor identified as closer to the apex. Today, the apex sits in the periphery and the world has irremediably changed since then. Indeed, this thinking makes us re-imagine the law starting from its core objectives and intimate meanings that sometimes push the "legal" boundaries if we want to build up new integrated and harmonised legal or quasi-legal systems. For example, as we said, alternative ways of investing represent alternative models of financing, either in the form of digital currencies (Bitcoin) or in the form of cash-shell vehicles and alternative acquisition models (SPACs). In both instances, the law does not play any substantive role in the form of an authoritarian form of state regulation, and financial markets appear – for the first time – to be democratised rather than liberalised through regulation and cross-border rules.

1.2 The Global Financial Crisis (2007–2010)

The financial crisis (2007–2010) has been defined as "the biggest crisis since the Great Depression".[13] It started pre-eminently as a mortgage-lending crisis in the United States,[14] although the diffusion of speculative derivative contracts traded on over-the-counter markets is identified as one of several causes.[15]

The lack of financial regulation and monitoring and the incorrect pricing of financial risk led to a fuelled credit bubble whose first fatal effects were seen in the collapse of the market for subprime mortgages in the United States. A subprime mortgage consists of a residential loan or mortgage issued to high-risk borrowers who face bankruptcy or have a late payment history (*i.e.* they are subprime borrowers). Therefore, the rate of interest charged to those borrowers was higher than that of a prime mortgage. Nonetheless, lenders such as banks sold – through a system of securitisation[16] – their credit to investors, who in turn became holders

---

-why-investors-fell-in-love-with-these-stock-market-vehicles-and-how-the-bubble-burst-162968, accessed on 3 July 2021.

13 Ioannis Kokkoris, Rodrigo Olivares-Caminal, *Antitrust Law Amidst Financial Crises* (1st edn, CUP 2010) 90. Although crises are seen as a recurrent feature of financial history (see Charles Kindleberger, *Manias, Panics and Crashes. A History of Financial Crises* (3rd edn, John Wiley & Dons 1996).

14 Indeed, there are multiple causes of the current economic crisis (see Glen Arnold, *Modern Financial Markets and Institutions – A Practical Perspective* (Pearson Education 2012) 660).

15 Lynn A. Stout, "Derivatives and the legal origin of the 2008 credit crisis" (2011) 1 Harvard Business Law Review 1, 7.

16 Yuliya Demyanyk, Otto Van Hemert, "Understanding the subprime mortgage crisis" (2011) 24 (6) The Review of Financial Studies 1848. For definition of terms see also "Definition of subprime", Financial Times Lexicon available at http://lexicon.ft.com/Term?term=subprime, accessed on 10 February 2015. The subprime mortgages were usually packed either into mortgage backed securities (MBSs) or collateralised mortgage obligations (CMOs), namely two different forms of asset-backed securities that use a mortgage or a pool of mortgages as collateral (see the definition of "mortgage-backed securities MBS", *Financial Times Lexicon*, available at http://lexicon.ft.com/Term?term=mortgage_backed-securities--MBS, accessed on 10 February 2015) and were sold to investors as a form of synthetic instrument having high-risk return prospects. In other words, if the

of asset-backed securities. In light of this, premiums paid on collaterals (*i.e.* mortgages/loans) were attractive on returns for asset-backed holders due to the higher interest rate, but the effective repayment of the principal of the mortgage would have been convenient for high-risk borrowers only in the case of an increase in house prices.

This form of speculation became even more aggressive when holders of asset-backed securities started entering into derivative contracts to bet on the loan performance in order to receive additional premiums in case of an increase in housing prices. This circumstance led to a speculation spiral when, between 2004 and 2006, house prices started to drop but debt itself was not downgraded.[17] As a result, defaults on subprime mortgages began to rise and triggered devaluation of housing-related securities, causing losses to financial intermediaries, raising prices on insurance for default, and reducing inter-bank lending.[18]

Before the crisis, the main instruments for financing the investment activities of private equity funds were inter-bank lending and lending activities generally.[19] The lack of strict regulatory requirements or direct supervision of financial intermediaries in some measure facilitated this process, especially in the European Union.[20]

When the crisis hit financial markets, the high reliance on debt securities (such as loans, bonds, etc.) diminished, and there was rising financial panic. For instance, the notorious collapse of one of the most important investment banks in 2007 (Lehman Brothers)[21] brought further deterioration to the economic conditions of the financial environment and gave rise to concerns in relation to moral hazard and the feasibility of bailout procedures.[22] Hence, the new volatility of

---

value of houses had continued to increase, reimbursement of the original loan that constituted the underlying asset of the MBS or the CMO would have been likely to occur.

17 Niamh Moloney, "EU financial market regulation after the global financial crisis: 'More Europe' or more risks?" (2010) 47 (5) Common Market Law Review 1317, 1319.

18 This circumstance is also often defined as a credit crunch (see Jorgen Elmeskov, "The general economic background of the crisis" (OCDE 2009), available at www.oecd.org/eco/42843570.pdf, accessed on 10 February 2015.

19 Stephen Valdez, Philip Molyneux, *An Introduction to Global Financial Markets* (8th edn, Palgrave Macmillan 2016) 39.

20 Moloney (n 17) 1319. Indeed, she highlights how "additional difficulties beset the EU, arising from the mis-match between the pan-EU operations of some major banking groups and nationally-based supervision and resolution regimes (...) at the core of the EU crisis was a destructive imbalance in the regulatory and supervisory architecture. The regulatory structure facilitated the cross-border activities of the large EU groups which had supported integration of the banking market, but it did not adequately address cross-border supervision, co-ordination, crisis resolution, and deposit protection".

21 Arnold (n 14) 660; Jennifer Hughes, "The Bad Dread Team Part I – II" (2008 November) Financial Times.

22 It is the well-known argument "too-big-to-fail". See Rosa Lastra, "Crisis management" in *International Financial and Monetary Law* (2nd edn, OUP 2015) 154; Kenneth Ayotte, David Skeel, "Bankruptcy or bailouts?" (2010) 35 Journal of Corporation Law 35; also before the current crisis (2007–2010) some arguments for bailout procedures and its effect were taken into account (see

financial markets called into doubt whether central banks should have been in charge of financial stability as a whole in addition to their traditional monetary stability role,[23] although central banks were in a position to foresee the 2007–2010 financial crisis, due to the well-known phenomenon of high leverage and under-pricing of risk (the narrow mandate).[24] The crisis led to a rethinking of the classic role of central banks and the need for central banks to regulate banks[25] and other financial intermediaries,[26] as well as to focus attention on international financial conglomerates, due to the possible spill-over effect and systemic risk[27] that can be caused by their fatal collapse.[28] Hence, the GFC and financial stability considerations led to the expansion of the Central Bank's LOLR function, and monetary authority, and added new responsibilities in macro and microprudential supervision. The role of Central Banks as crisis managers acquired a new dimension. Think of 2009, when the Bank of England introduced a new monetary policy tool called "quantitative easing" to inject liquidity into the economy.[29]

In 2008, the crisis moved fast to the real economy, evolving into a recession and affecting households, businesses, and jobs.[30] Price fluctuation, it has been noted, is likely to impact the real economy because the housing market is also part of a "credit-fuelled asset price bubble"[31] where prices can drop, but private

---

Gerard Caprio, Daniela Klingebiel, "Bank insolvency: Bad luck, bad policy, or bad banking?" (1997) *Annual World Bank Conference on Development Economics* 79).

23 Howard Davies, David Green, *Banking on the Future: The Fall and Rise of Central Banking* (Princeton University Press 2010) 52.

24 Charles Goodhart, *The Regulatory Response to the Financial Crisis* (Edward Elgar 2009) 9. Goodhart highlights that it was clearly perceivable from financial stability reviews published by central banks that "differentials between risky assets and safe assets (...) declined to historically low levels. Volatility was unusually low. Leverage was high, as financial institutions sought to add to yield, in the face of very low interest rates".

25 Charles Goodhart, *The Evolution of Central Banks* (1988 MIT Press) 85.

26 Valdez, Molyneux (n 19) 27. One of the main concerns of the current financial crisis is focused on the phenomenon referred to as the shadow banking system, namely institutions that are not properly banks, but that carry out all the activities commonly referred to a bank or clearing house.

27 In the aftermath of the crisis, financial regulation has highlighted the need to regulate and identify systematically important financial institutions (SIFIs). See Valdez, Molyneux (n 19) 128.

28 Rosa Lastra, Rodrigo Olivares-Caminal, "Cross-border insolvency: The case of financial conglomerates" in John Raymond Labrosse et al. (eds), *Financial Crisis Management and Bank Resolution* (Informa 2009) 269; additionally, it should be highlighted that the collapse of an international financial conglomerate or complex financial group, as well as the global dimension of financial markets, manifests the need for resolution and rethinking of cross-border bank insolvency; see Rosa Lastra, "International law principles applicable to cross-border bank insolvency" in Rosa Lastra (ed), *Cross-Border Bank Insolvency* (OUP 2011) 161.

29 House of Lords – Economic Affairs Committee, "Quantitative easing: a dangerous addiction?" (16 July 2021), available at https://committees.parliament.uk/publications/6725/documents/71894/default/, accessed on 10 November 2021.

30 Stephen Figlewski, "Viewing the financial crisis from 20,000 feet up" (2009) 16 Journal of Derivatives 53, 56.

31 Richard W. Vague, Robert C. Hockett, "Debt, deflation, and debacle: Of private debt write-down and public recovery" (2013) available at http://works.bepress.com/robert_hockett/48/, accessed on 17 October 2016 and 5 January 2021.

debt loads simply cannot. For this reason, private debt has been identified as the main trigger for failure cascades and detrimental spill-over effects.

The world economy has been reshaped by the 2007–2010 crisis,[32] which has manifested negative widespread effects on the whole economy (*i.e.* systemic risk and contagion)[33] due to the internationalisation of financial markets.[34]

The 2007–2010 economic crisis stands apart from previous crises, which were seen as a successful test for the economy and were confined to certain sectors of financial markets, due to its "super-bubble nature", involving every sector of the financial markets.[35] As a result, financial markets still show a lack of confidence and efficiency. The economic effects of the financial crisis affect investor confidence due to information asymmetry and agency costs issues, whereas managers and financial intermediaries see them in terms of systemic risk and contagion due to moral hazard concerns. Establishing a new legal and economic order, namely a new "paradigm" in financial markets[36] has become a necessity, where scepticism and distrust are present in each financial operation, especially borrowing and bank or inter-bank lending.

Summing up, it can be said that the 2007–2010 financial crisis is the welfare cost of under-priced private debt, where the social consequences in terms of unemployment and human dignity have far overwhelmed the classic concerns of macroeconomic entities such as inflationary or deflationary processes. To this end, the notion of systemic risk has become vital for a correct understanding of financial markets today, but the lack of an agreed definition of systemic risk[37] can give rise to both dogmatic and practical issues in terms of governance of

---

32 Arnold (n 14) 659; although some authors have argued the opposite view see Suzanne Konzelmann, Marc Fovargue-Davies, Olivier Butzbach, "The 'not so global' crisis" in Suzanne Knozelmann, Marc Fovargue-Davies (eds), *Banking Systems in the Crisis – The Faces of Liberal Capitalism* (Routledge 2013) 1; on the global crisis argument see also Alan Rechtschaffen, Jean-Claude Trichet, *Capital Markets, Derivatives and the Law: Evolution After the Crisis* (OUP 2014) 3–4.

33 Lastra, *International Financial and Monetary Law* (n 22) 179; Jean Helwege, Caiyan Zhang, "Financial Firm Bankruptcy and Contagion" (2013) Midwest Finance Association 2013 Annual Meeting Paper 1, 3.

34 Indeed, the internationalisation of capital markets started with petro-dollar recycling in the 1970s, but reached its peak in the 1990s after the economic reforms of Thatcher in the UK and Reagan in the United States. See Arnold (n 14) 659; Ravi Tennekoon, *The Law and Regulation of International Finance* (LexisNexis 1991).

35 George Soros, *The New Paradigm for Financial Markets – The Credit Crisis of 2008 and What It Means* (Public Affairs 2008) 100. In the author's view, the super-bubble hypothesis "could be used to create a comprehensive financial history of the post-World War II period, culminating in the current crisis".

36 Ibid, 12.

37 Alexander Kern, Dhumale Rahul, Eatwell John, *Global Governance of Financial Systems: The International Regulation of Systemic Risk* (OUP 2006) 24–33. The authors mention the work of Dow (2000) according to whom the concept of systemic risk deals with the failure of a payment and settlement system or with a type of financial failure that induces a macroeconomic crisis. In addition, other studies (Cranston, 1996) have identified systemic risk as an inherent feature of international banking in order to include global systemic risk, safety and solvency risks that arise from lending activities, and risk to depositors through the lack of bank insurance.

financial markets and prevention of epidemic spill-over effects. For this reason, the main feature to highlight is the understanding of systemic risk as a product of the mispricing of financial risk, through which private actors who create financial risk do not internalise its cost but spread it on to society. In other words, this is a new connotation of financial risk as a form of negative externality, or pollution.[38]

1.2.1 Risk and Uncertainty

We have outlined before how in the view of Pistor, liquidity shortage in financial markets can be qualified in terms of uncertainty and therefore crisis when new financing cannot be secured; essentially, any crisis is triggered by uncertainty. Additionally, it is intuitive to assert that any financial crisis is based on the assumption that the system is already pre-coded and destined to fail or collapse. This view of uncertainty is very distant from an economic point of view. Indeed, according to Frank Knight, one of the most prominent American economists of the last century, uncertainty underpins money creation processes rather than undermining them.

In contemporary financial markets, risk is an objective feature of markets, and it is understood under what I define as the "human-humanity" paradigm.[39] However, risk must be contextualised within markets if we want to discover its ontological meaning. Specifically, the qualification of financial risk is explained by the constant interrelation between savers (*i.e.* lenders) and users (*i.e.* borrowers) that shapes the structure of financial markets.[40] The financial market is where the different assets of interest of lenders and borrowers are matched. Specifically, lenders aim to be risk-averse, whereas borrowers are essentially risk-takers, and they are more aggressive because they strive for profit.

This work also aims to theorise financial markets under a Luhmannian paradigm of system theory,[41] where the observation of markets defines them as financial systems. However, the most challenging aspect of theorising financial markets as financial systems is to explain the structures of those systems. Four main structures can be identified in the markets, namely risk, uncertainty, competition, and financial innovations (see Chapter 3).

1.2.2 The Role of the Law in Financial Crisis

The primary objective of financial markets is not creating equality, but efficiently allocating resources. Those who have resources (the lenders) are interested in finding an efficient allocation through those who need them (the borrowers).

---

38 Ibid, 24.
39 See Chapter 3, and Daniele D'Alvia, "Risk, uncertainty and the market: A rethinking of Islamic and Western finance" (2020) 16 International Journal of Law in Context 339.
40 Valdez, Molyneux (n 19), 2.
41 Niklas Luhmann, *Introduction to Systems Theory* (Polity Press 2013) 26.

According to this view, the role of the law must not be to interfere in the allocation of resources, but rather it must ensure that this activity is facilitated, and information is shared between those parties (namely, lenders and borrowers) transparently and accurately to avoid or at least mitigate the existence of under- or over-valued financial assets, fraud, and misstatements.[42] The possibility of a mispriced financial asset is high, not only because of the inefficient role of financial markets or the inattention or distraction of financial regulators but because of the subjective intimate structure of markets: the speculator's choices are determined under uncertain circumstances.

In 1936, the liberal British economist John Maynard Keynes in his influential work "The General Theory of Employment, Interest, and Money" introduced an economic theory that argued that government management of the economy could smooth out the highs and lows of the business cycle to produce more or less consistent growth with minimal unemployment. Keynes was one of the first economists to understand that financial markets are not only dominated by an objective conception of risk but that a subjective feature of risk is still vital for their functioning. Indeed, financial speculation (from Latin "speculum" – "mirror"), as opposed to investment, is based on a subjective belief in order to become profitable. Keynes confirmed this understanding by pointing out the difference between the knowable in principle and the necessarily unknowable. What is knowable in principle refers to our conception of risk, but the necessarily unknowable refers to this new subjective feature of capital markets. On this point, Keynes compared financial markets to a beauty contest. Here, the judges, instead of focusing their attention on the winner – the most beautiful girl – try to second guess the opinion of other judges. In the same way, in capital markets, speculators tend to focus their efforts not on the objective reality of the financial assets being sold or offered on the market, but on the information that other speculators will trade on in the near future. Hence, the evaluation of financial assets is not only based on an assessment of the past performance of assets but on the uncertainty of the decision that will be taken by other speculators. To state it plainly, the objective discourse on risk does not apply alone in capital markets because there will be always a subjective component in the final decision of the speculator. This trade on information before somebody else trades on the same information is vital for unwinding positions early and it is also essential for setting the price of the financial asset.[43] In this game, the value of information for a speculator depends on the uncertain behaviour of another speculator (necessarily unknowable). In addition, because the markets will always present a lack of perfect information (*i.e.* information asymmetry), basing the value of financial assets on new or erroneous information might lead to mispriced assets. Hence, even a speculator in good faith can affect

---

42 Here we take into account a broad definition of financial assets that include bonds, stocks, commodities, and financial innovation.

43 Markus K. Brunnermeier, *Asset Pricing under Asymmetric Information, Bubbles, Crashes, Technical Analysis, and Herding* (OUP 2001).

the value of financial assets in a negative way. This is why supervision of financial markets is required, but it cannot definitively solve the issue.[44]

The role of law in contemporary financial markets has dramatically changed. Law is not the input, but the output, and self-regulation (or indirect soft law), as well as market practices and contractual arrangements, constitute a new decentralised system where the figure of a central planner is absent, and the role of law is notably modified.

1.2.3 The 2020 Unfolding Crisis: Covid-19

The recession caused by the Covid-19 pandemic is one of the worst global recessions in modern times. Back in March 2020, the International Monetary Fund warned that in light of Covid-19, the expectations of a deep global recession were almost certain.[45]

As a result of the crisis, many businesses needed to restructure both operationally and financially. Because of Covid-19 some of those businesses had to be liquidated. The crisis quickly moved from the corporate sector, especially small and medium enterprises, with losses of output, redundancies, and some closures, to public finances, where pressure became enormous. This is true especially in developing countries that were already highly indebted. The internal situation of businesses in those countries has also often been compromised. The insolvency law frameworks of those countries do not always recognise new development trends in insolvency practices that, today, are based on business rescue, out-of-court arrangements (private workouts), and preventive restructuring (see Section 1.3). For example, in Ecuador, formal insolvency proceedings have traditionally been the only alternative to liquidation recognised by the Ecuadorian insolvency framework. And even the recent Humanitarian Act enacted by Ecuador as a response to the current economic crisis generated by the pandemic allowing debtors and creditors to negotiate their facility agreements presents many downsides including, *inter alia*, the lack of a moratorium period to facilitate such negotiations between debtors and creditors. This is not an isolated case, and legal proceedings in emerging markets are usually value-destroying for debtors and creditors.[46] To this end, out-of-court reorganisation agreements (private workouts) could be an efficient alternative to formal insolvency proceedings. As the World Bank Group[47] has argued, in times of Covid-19, informal reorganisation agreements, due to their

---

44 Goodhart (n 25).

45 Kristalina Georgieva, "Transcript of press briefing by Kristalina Georgieva following a conference call on the International Monetary and Financial Committee" (27 March 2020), IMF, available at www.imf.org/en/News/Articles/2020/03/27/tr032720-transcript-press-briefing-kristalina-georgieva-following-imfc-conference-call, accessed on 20 June 2021.

46 Aurelio Gurrea-Martinez, "Insolvency law in emerging markets" (10 June 2021) Ibero-American Institute for Law and Finance, Working Paper 3/2020.

47 World Bank Group, "Covid-19 outbreak: Implications on corporate and individual insolvency" (13 April 2020) available at https://pubdocs.worldbank.org/en/912121588018942884/COVID

flexibility, will contribute in a less time-consuming way towards rescuing viable companies.

Looking at the growing indebtedness of developing countries, the World Bank, the International Monetary Fund, and the United Nations launched various initiatives to relieve the public debt burden in the unusual situation triggered by Covid-19. A first step was established when the G20 countries agreed to grant a moratorium on official bilateral debt of the world's 76 poorest economies (the Debt Service Suspension Initiative to cover the official debts of poor countries). Since it took effect on 1 May 2020, the initiative has delivered more than $5 billion in relief to more than 40 eligible countries.[48] The suspension period, originally set to end on 31 December 2020, has been extended through to December 2021. Borrowers under the debt service suspension initiative (DSSI) scheme commit to using freed-up resources to increase health, social, or economic spending in response to the pandemic crisis. Specifically, the approach of the G20 to the pandemic follows the six principles of the Paris Club.[49] These include solidarity, consensus, and information sharing among the Club members, including participation on a voluntary basis by private and multilateral creditors. These are the foundations of the DSSI. Furthermore, due to the initial limited operability of the DSSI, in November 2020, the G20 announced an agreed "Common Framework for Debt Treatments beyond the Debt Service Suspension Initiative". This framework includes the G20 and the Paris Club and requires domestic approval by all the participants; it aims to address the problem of unsustainable debt based on an IMF and World Bank debt sustainability analysis. The framework requires countries to seek similar treatment from private creditors in nominal, net-present-value, and duration terms.

Those historical reforms tested the international financial architecture. "Sustainability" became a term that is now ubiquitous in global finance and investment. Indeed, the principles embodied in the UN Sustainable Development Goals are devoted to building a better world. Those principles are deeply relevant when it comes to the sovereign debt of struggling developing countries. For example, in February 2020, before the Covid-19 crisis became acute, the IMF concluded[50] that Argentina's public debt is "unsustainable". Indeed, debt sustainability was increasingly at risk even before the Covid-19 crisis: out of 69 countries applying

---

-19-Outbreak-Implications-on-Corporate-and-Individual-Insolvency.pdf, accessed on 10 August 2021.

48 World Bank, "Covid-19: Debt service suspension initiative" (18 June 2021) Brief, available at www.worldbank.org/en/topic/debt/brief/covid-19-debt-service-suspension-initiative, accessed on 13 July 2021.

49 Paris Club, "The six principles" available at https://clubdeparis.org/en/communications/page/the-six-principles, accessed on 14 July 2021.

50 IMF, "IMF staff statement on Argentina" (19 February 2020), available at www.imf.org/en/News/Articles/2020/02/19/pr2057-argentina-imf-staff-statement-on-argentina, accessed on 18 June 2021.

the Low-Income Countries Debt Sustainability Analysis in 2019, half were either already in debt distress or at high risk of debt distress, against 23% in 2013.[51]

As a result, debt sustainability for low-income economies and debt relief became the most attractive ways to combat the pandemic. Furthermore, climate change and falling biodiversity have become a new trigger to justify reforms in a sovereign debt crisis. In light of this, the example of Barbados is self-explanatory. Back in 2018–2019, during its debt restructuring, Barbados exchanged old debt with natural disaster clauses. Under these clauses, when an international organisation such as the World Health Organisation declares a natural disaster, the debt service is immediately suspended for two years. At a first glance, natural disaster clauses can provide an immediate instrument to secure debt relief in the event of a natural disaster, including a pandemic. However, as has been authoritatively outlined,[52] it is controversial which developing countries can be allowed to use a natural disaster clause and which cannot. One size does not fit all, especially if we consider larger developing economies.

Climate change and sustainability is a new challenge for the financial ecosystem that is possibly preparing the ground to broaden the mandates of Central Banks too. For instance, within the Central Bank monetary policy mandate, the importance of implementing a green quantitative easing, or within micro-prudential supervision by following ESG criteria to sanction unsustainable activities (such as lending linked to deforestation), and finally in terms of macroprudential supervision the application of macroprudential tools to carbon markets. Whether this move is a useful addition to curtail environmental challenges and help sustainable businesses to soar, it is difficult to assess. The world is too interconnected and complex today to express a final judgement on this new trend, but surely it is a remarkable transformation where non-legal words such as sustainability are even affecting financial tools in monetary and supervision policies.

From those examples, it is evident that the Covid-19 crisis has dramatically contributed to a speedy reshaping of the outlook of the international financial architecture in its search for less cumbersome debt restructuring procedures, debt suspensions, and moratoriums, and its orientation towards flexible paradigms of the law that necessarily sit far beyond the purposes of a codification of the law as "input" in Pistor's terms. Similarly, debt restructuring in private businesses is taking the form of out-of-court reorganisation agreements between debtors and their creditors (see Section 1.3).

---

51 International Monetary Fund, "The evolution of public debt vulnerabilities in lower income economies" (February 2020) IMF Policy Paper.
52 Rodrigo Olivares-Caminal, Paola Subacchi, "Letter: Barbados debt relief model is hard to extend to all poor states" (8 July 2021) Financial Times, available at www.ft.com/content/ef2f6603-66bb-47fe-83ba-fcbe5a61a5a1, accessed on 13 July 2021.

1.3 The Evolution of Corporate Insolvency Law Regimes

In the previous sections, we briefly touched upon the imperfection of traditional insolvency law tools in handling the distress of complex cross-border banks with the Lehman example, and we outlined how the absence of an international legal framework for sovereign-debt restructuring can prevent indebted countries from recovering. The system cannot afford continuous bailouts and debt relief measures, therefore, the stability of the financial system seems to be inherently compromised. The EU bank resolution regime in Europe, for instance, can be understood as a possible answer to this criticality. Since then, the banking system has undergone fundamental changes. However, the same cannot be said for the rules applicable to non-financial enterprises (see Section 1.3.1). For instance, focusing on corporate insolvency regimes, it is extremely controversial whether general principles exist within the EU legal order. Corporate insolvency law comprises an array of interests and constitutes the resulting balance of several objectives. On the one hand, it represents the main protection of creditors' interests as well as the counter-tool to rebalance shareholders' limited liability safeguard (namely, the possibility to liquidate a non-viable company).

Globally, since 2009, there has been a significant level of insolvency law reform. These reforms were triggered by the 2007–2010 GFC and subsequent economic downturn. In 2010, INSOL Europe produced a report on the harmonisation levels of insolvency laws in the European Union.[53] The report identified that the EU's diverse legal environment created disparity among member states and incentivised forum-shopping. This unbalanced legal environment did not go unnoticed. There was an attempt in 2014 by the European Commission Recommendation to Member States,[54] but its non-binding nature did not produce changes at national level. In 2015, the European Union amended the EC Insolvency Regulation[55] concerning the rules of jurisdiction for opening insolvency proceedings in the EU with the Recast Insolvency Regulation, which underlined the need for cooperation and communication between insolvency offer holders to explore the possibility of restructuring and the implementation of a restructuring plan (art. 41).[56] Subsequently, in 2016, the European Commission adopted its proposal for a Directive on Preventive Restructuring Frameworks to increase the efficiency of restructuring, insolvency, and discharge procedures, amending Directive

---

53 INSOL Europe, "Harmonisation of insolvency law at EU level", European Parliament, Directorate General for International Policies, Policy Department C: Citizens' Rights and Constitutional Affairs (2010) Legal Affairs, PE 419.633.

54 European Commission, Recommendation (COM (2014) 1500 final).

55 Regulation (EC) No. 1346/2000 OJ L 160 (30 June 2000) 1.

56 OJ L 141 (5 June 2015) 19.

2012/30/EU.[57] Since then, the first discussions on early restructuring, cram-down, new financing, and the debtor-in-possession have taken place.[58]

On 20 June 2019, the European Parliament and the Council published in the Official Journal of the European Union the text of Directive 2019/1023 on preventing restructuring frameworks, discharge of debt and disqualifications, and measures to increase the efficiency of procedures concerning restructuring, insolvency, and discharged debt, amending Directive (EU) 2017/1132 (the Restructuring Directive).[59] This needs to be implemented into national law by 17 July 2021, subject to a one-year extension.

The Restructuring Directive establishes the tools for the establishment of a more harmonised and effective debt restructuring framework among member states that will provide insolvent or over-indebted companies with the opportunity to continue their business operations with the possibility of regaining debt sustainability within a reasonable time period. The objective of eliminating the possible differences of the various debt restructuring procedures across member states creates a more transparent and predictable system as creditors, investors, employees, and shareholders will be familiar with the solutions available in a potential distress situation of a debtor across the Union. For this reason, it has been noted that for many decades, Europe (although not a federation) has not been known for its debtor or restructuring friendly insolvency practice.[60] Unlike the regime under Chapter 11 of the US Bankruptcy Code, Europe has taken longer to adapt its legal frameworks to facilitate restructuring procedures.

The Restructuring Directive is timely due to the urgency imposed by the unfolding crisis triggered by Covid-19, which in some instances has already constituted a remarkable reformulation of the law. However, some provisions of the Directive, such as the cross-class cram-down provisions, are likely to be less easy to implement in emerging economies that have less sophisticated institutional frameworks, and where it is already a challenge to shift the focus towards insolvency as a tool for restructuring. Furthermore, the pandemic is an opportunity to incentivise the adoption of national corporate restructuring frameworks that can provide viable businesses with new financing and restructuring tools such as cram-down mechanisms and debtor-in-possession procedures but also simplifying the applicable rules for SMEs.

57　European Commission, "Proposal for a Directive on preventive restructuring frameworks, second chance and measures to increase the efficiency of restructuring, insolvency and discharge procedures and amending Directive 2012/30/EU". Strasbourg (22 November 2016) COM (2016) 723 final.

58　Gerard McCormack, "Corporate restructuring law – a second chance for Europe?" (2017) 42 (4) E.L. Rev. 532.

59　Directive (EU) 2019/1023 of the European Parliament and of the Council of 20 June 2019 on preventing restructuring frameworks, insolvency, and discharge of debt, and amending Directive (EU) 2017/1132 (Directive on restructuring and insolvency) OJ L 172.

60　David Christoph Ehmke, Jennifer L Gant, et al., "The European Union Preventive Restructuring Framework: A hole in one?" (2019) 28 (2) International Insolvency Review 184.

Insolvency proceedings tend to be country-specific, as most of their rules have a re-distributive impact on a broad range of stakeholders of the company such as employees, creditors, and customers. Hence, insolvency law regimes are mainly related to political balances and national social security policies.

The main idea of the Restructuring Directive is that debtors in financial difficulty but not yet insolvent can avail themselves of restructuring and that national authorities should order a general stay of individual enforcement actions.

Corporate insolvency law – as it can be seen – is a powerful mechanism to promote economic growth. It works in two ways: *ex ante*, a well-functioning insolvency framework can simplify and facilitate innovation, entrepreneurship, and access to finance; *ex post*, corporate insolvency law can perform several functions, including the reorganisation of viable companies in financial distress, the liquidation of non-viable businesses in a fair and efficient manner, and the maximisation of returns to creditors. This means that an efficient insolvency framework is essential for any economy and even more for emerging economies, where there is a lack of developed capital markets that make it harder for firms to have access to finance. As we said before, capital markets are the main venue where different and opposite interests meet to find an efficient allocation of resources. In light of this, firms and corporations rely on capital markets to access finance either with the issuance of equity in the form of traditional IPOs, legitimate alternative paths to traditional IPOs (SPACs and direct listing), or debt through corporate bonds (essentially, private debt).

1.3.1 The Private and Public Divide in Insolvency Law

Instability in the corporate and banking sectors and at the central government level can lead to a "doomed loop" (or vicious cycle). However, the protection of interests or – as Pistor would prefer – the codification of interests can vary between banking resolution regimes and corporate rescue and cross-border insolvency. This is because bank insolvency is focused on macroprudential objectives to preserve financial stability; on the other hand, insolvency law in relation to non-financial entities has always been centred on a) micro-prudential objectives; b) contractarian theories centred on coordinating problems of creditors' bargains; and c) post-crisis liquidation of assets among creditors.[61]

Non-financial entities do not create systemic risk, at least in theory. This theoretical distinction between entity-centric insolvency law and systemic public-interest-oriented bank resolutions works well for relatively small non-financial entities, however,[62] it gives rise to issues in relation to significant non-financial enterprises. Indeed, the failure of a multinational corporation or a state-link group

---

61 Ilya Kokorin, "Insolvency of significant non-financial enterprises: Lessons from bank failures and bank resolution" (24 May 2020) Hazelhoff Research Paper Series No. 10.
62 Robert E Scott, "Through bankruptcy with the creditors' bargain heuristic" (1996) 53 (2) The University of Chicago Law Review 690.

can create systemic risk as much as a bank failure does. Hence, the collapse of significant non-financial enterprises can require state intervention and, at the same time, out-of-court proceedings might facilitate the rescue of viable business entities. Evergrande is a self-evident example. In October 2021, once a symbol of success and the embodiment of the incredible growth of China's real estate sector over the past 20 years, Mr. Hui Ka Yan (the founder of Evergrande) today faces a stunning reversal of fortunes. Evergrande has been on the brink of default with more than $300bn of total liabilities and having missed interest payments on bonds in September 2021, it sparked China's biggest debt restructuring. This gave rise to the argument on whether the Chinese government should step in to provide financial support to the company with similar grounds to a "too-big-to-fail" doctrine in bank insolvency. The Chinese government took the distance because taxpayers' money as in bank runs is too precious to be used to fuel a period of political instability. To our ends, what matters is that non-financial entities can also contribute to systemic risk. Evergrande created a mounting spillover risk that soon was spread to other corporations such as the Chinese Estates Holding (CEH), a Hong Kong-based property group. CEH announced an offer to take the business private after its exposure to heavily indebted Evergrande crushed its share price.[63] Evergrande is also our best example to provide evidence of the important role of foreign investors. One of the main issues with Evergrande was focused on delaying interest payment of bondholders. The missed payments trigged a 30-day grace period before the company formally defaults. This potentially could have paved the way for a group of investors with sufficient holding of the bonds to take legal action. Yet Evergrande survived in October 2021 because the company timely repaid at least the missed interest payment and avoided a formal default. Once again Evergrande was still the debtor-in-possession and work resumed in real estate projects in China. Nonetheless, new evils emerged, such as a massive delay of payment of salaries to "pump" indirectly liquidity into the income statement, and *dulcis in fundo* in November 2021, China's top banking regulator (the China Banking and Insurance Regulatory Commission) started an investigation into the relationship between Evergrande and a little-known Chinese regional bank (Shengjing Bank) it part-owned. This is posing a new threat to the world's most indebted property group and its billionaire founder Mr Hui Ka Yan. As can be seen, liquidity crises can be fast turned into an insolvency issue and formal default. Beyond foreign investors' concerns, operational risk matters, and it is difficult to regulate this market risk away (see Chapter 3).

During the outbreak of Covid-19, the implementation of rigid governmental measures to curb the pandemic has affected many businesses, in particular those dependent on global supply chains, travel, and liquidity flows (such as car rentals, airlines, automotive manufacturing, etc.). It is not by chance that Norwegian Air, Hertz, and LATAM Airlines Group had to file for insolvency or restructuring – the

---

63 Thomas Hale, Primrose Riordan, "Evergrande shareholder to delist in Hong Kong as contagion hits stock" (7 October 2021) Financial Times.

process in which several jurisdictions and courts were engaged. However, historically, as we said before, the handling of financial distress and the application of insolvency law mechanisms have been carried out on a single-jurisdiction and a single-entity level. Wider group context was often overlooked. Insolvency law rules, as well as company law provisions, were mainly focused on a single-entity/ single-debtor process lacking provisions related to groups of companies. Today, this approach has been dramatically reformed in relation to enterprise groups in the emergence of soft law instruments, which target the insolvency of corporate groups. For example, the rules and recommendations addressing enterprise group insolvency and resolution of credit institutions (e.g. the Bank Recovery and Resolution Directive (BRRD): although the BRRD does not use the term "group solution", it promotes group resolvability where a banking group should be allowed to fail in an orderly manner without adverse consequences on financial stability), the Recast Insolvency Regulation that we mentioned in the previous section, and the UNCITRAL Model Law on Enterprise Group Insolvency[64] in 2019. These soft law instruments and hard law rules show that the concept of a group solution is flexible, and the form of the law must be flexible too and contained in guidelines and de-centralised models of law. The definition of the flexibility of a group solution reflects the possibility of taking into account the circumstances of a specific enterprise group, its business model, and its degree of integration between group members.

To this end, there are different tools that can facilitate a group solution, one, for instance, being the conclusion of cross-border insolvency protocols (think of the one used in LATAM Airlines and Urbancorp Group), the appointment of the same insolvency practitioner in separate insolvency proceedings of group members, the extension of an enforcement stay to group entities, and so on. One common understanding is that in the absence of a substantive group consolidation, group entities retain their legal separateness in insolvency, and creditors' pre-insolvency entitlements should be protected.

At first sight, it seems that the debtor-centric approach must prevail in the absence of a group solution definition. However, the complexity of contemporary insolvency with specific regard to a group solution can be achieved through the implementation of various tools and mechanisms that vary from jurisdiction to jurisdiction and are strongly influenced by societal goals. For example, on 14 May 2021, there was a new chapter in cross-border insolvency, namely the first application by Hong Kong liquidators for recognition and assistance in Mainland China. A cooperation mechanism was established between Mainland China and Hong Kong in the form of the "Record of Meeting of the Supreme People's Court and the Government of the Hong Kong Special Administrative Region and Mutual Recognition of and Assistance to Bankruptcy (Insolvency) Proceedings between

---

64 United Nations – Commission on International Trade Law, "UNCITRAL model law on enterprise group insolvency with guide to enactment" (2019), available at https://uncitral.un.org/en/MLEGI, accessed on 15 August 2021.

the Court of the Mainland and the Hong Kong Special Administrative Region". In accordance with this cooperation mechanism, the Mainland China and Hong Kong jurisdictions agreed to terms where pilot cities (Shanghai, Shenzhen, and Xiamen) on the Mainland and Hong Kong would mutually recognise and assist each other in insolvency matters. The very first application has been recently issued by the Hong Kong Companies Court to the Bankruptcy Court of the Shenzhen Intermediate People's Court in *Re Samson Paper Company Limited (in Creditors' Voluntary Liquidation)* [2021] HKCFI 2151. The introduction of the cooperation mechanism is the beginning of the removal of an all too common obstacle encountered by insolvency practitioners in Hong Kong, and its timely implementation goes well with the anticipated increase in cross-border economic interaction in the foreseeable future.

These examples show that today the private and public divide in insolvency law proceedings has vanished, and the flexibility of definitions necessarily leads to a peripheric system of law rather than a centric one. In other words, the installation of a central planner has lost its appeal, the law is less abstract, and it appears to be oriented towards practical solutions and cooperation mechanisms that, in insolvency law proceedings, for instance, can find application in a myriad of insolvency and pre-insolvency tools rather than in pre-codified and codified instruments. This is because complexity is seen as a means of creating order, and in insolvency practices, order is not always connected to the global level but can and should be first achieved locally. Only in this way can the local order influence the establishment of a global order in a new integration of global and local.

1.3.2 Contractarian and Out-of-Law Approaches

In the previous section, we introduced and provided preliminary reflections on the de-centralised role of the law. This necessarily implies a rethinking of the enforcement of the law as well as imagining out-of-law approaches. Again, in insolvency law proceedings, this is directly reflected in the continuous conflict and contrast between court-supervised mechanisms and out-of-law tools.

From the 1980s to the present day, increasing numbers of companies have found themselves in default or having to deal with insolvency procedures.[65] There has been a striking debate that has arisen in the last few decades mainly due to the need to resolve corporate distress in an efficient and resolutive manner. The major concern, when a company is in distress, is reassuring the creditors by stating that the value of their claims will not diminish. However, the process of corporate distress is both inevitable and a desired outcome for a market, which can be seen as strong in its entirety. Concurrently, the major increase in insolvency procedures has resulted in striking innovations in this field. Some of the most notable ones

---

65 Sris Chatterjee, Upinder S. Dhillon, Gabriel G. Ramirez, "Resolution of financial distress: Debt restructurings via Chapter 11, Pre-packaged Bankruptcies, and Workouts" (1996) 25 (1) Financial Management 5.

are pre-packaged and pre-negotiated bankruptcies. This has amounted to a better understanding of financial distress as a feature that can arise in companies.[66]

In other words, one of the most challenging decisions that company directors have to make when their company is in distress is whether and at what stage to involve the court. Indeed, the insolvency of a company can have two judicial consequences: first, the company can be liquidated in order to pay its creditors through a process that ends with the disposal of the company's assets in auction sales in order to disinterest its creditors. Usually, the management and the shareholders lose control over the company, which is driven by an independent judicial liquidator who ensures the proper progress of the liquidation. This solution is only envisioned as a last resort because through this route a company's financial health is irretrievably compromised. Indeed, if the distress is severe enough and the company is at a "point of no return" (see the *Eurosail* case), directors have no choice. However, the company can be rescued and have a second option through a judicial reorganisation. Here, the goal is to save the company's business when it is not compromised to a critical extent. Judicial reorganisations generally concern companies that have a chance to survive if solutions are found to diminish their indebtedness. The purpose of the proceeding is to offer the company a healthy break in order to restructure its debt, liabilities, and activities and pay its creditors. Judicial proceedings often come with an order from the court to impose stays on creditors' rights and attachments in order for the company to have time to organise the sale without being threatened by constant litigation. They appear at first glance a very effective solution for creditors to retrieve their money. The insolvency practitioners appointed by the courts will – for instance – focus on developing the most fruitful activities of companies and freeze those that are unprofitable. In liquidation processes, the goal is to end up with the best possible sale of the company's assets to pay all creditors in the end, and after this reorganisation, the company should be able to continue its activity.

However, a court-supervised reorganisation might not be the desirable answer for debtors, especially in times of crisis. For instance, the financial crisis triggered by the pandemic is having a major impact on economic activity around the globe and is still unfolding, producing devastating consequences for the economy and its players (see Chapter 3). As a result of the crisis, many businesses will need to restructure, both operationally and financially. Unlike in-court insolvency proceedings or supervised formal reorganisation procedures, out-of-court proceedings (known as private workouts) and hybrid procedures can effectively represent a cost-efficient solution to distressed business entities. A modern reorganisation law should facilitate access to business restructuring and provide for a plan to bind dissentient creditors and impose a minimum stay on execution over assets by creditors to facilitate a restructuring. At the same time, it should preserve the rights of creditors and the value of the assets that they could ultimately use for recovery.

---

66 Ibid.

The first consideration when deciding whether a court-supervised reorganisation or out-of-court private workout is preferable to restructuring the company is the importance of privacy. Insolvency information carries a negative stigma in the minds of the public. When a company initiates a court-supervised liquidation or restructuring opting for a judicial procedure, it can soon come to the knowledge of the public, which will in turn worsen the difficulties of the company in terms of its reputation. A company's partners and clients may be reluctant to continue their commercial relationships and the reconstruction of the company's assets is in consequence put at risk. In addition, all creditors are involved in these kinds of procedures and the chances for each one of them to retrieve their own money is reduced by dilution. For this reason, to keep financial difficulties undisclosed, companies tend to favour private agreements with their creditors in order to avoid any judicial intervention. These private agreements (private workouts) come in the form of contracts. Nonetheless, if the impact of knowledge of the financial situation is so great, this perhaps suggests market participants have the right to be aware of it. Transparency is important to the integrity and efficiency of financial markets and if shareholders and stakeholders lose confidence in the company, this is a consequence of the free market economy. The challenge is that it can be difficult to decipher how financially distressed a company truly is – many companies undergoing judicial supervised reorganisations are very successful, whereas some reveal that the only viable option may be liquidation. As recognised by the European Law Institute in a report in 2017 on "Rescue of Business in Insolvency Law", formal reorganisation still carries a stigma in many jurisdictions because it is associated with liquidation and the failure of a company. While there is an argument to be made that to address this stigma publicity should be encouraged, the reality remains that debtor companies prefer to keep reorganisations private for as long as possible. Workouts and pre-packages help them to achieve this and are preferred over judicial reorganisations.

However, the choice between out-of-court insolvency mechanisms (private workouts) and court-supervised business reorganisation is not a simple one and often depends on a case-by-case basis.

Definitively workouts are preferred in many cases. For example, a well-known non-liberal state such as China has started to modernise areas of its commercial law and has recently made use of private workouts to rescue an important company group. Indeed, China's courts increasingly take centre stage in managing complex restructurings and bankruptcy proceedings of failed conglomerates. This sets the scene for greater interaction with companies and investors, including foreign groups with interests in the world's second-biggest economy.[67] One example is the court-led restructuring of the Peking University Founder Group (PUFG) in 2021. In late 2019, PUFG offshore debts were about $38.5 billion. The restructuring of the group involved a consortium of strategic investors taking

---

67 Edward White, "China's courts take centre stage as defaults shake $17tn bond market" (24 August 2021) Financial Times.

over the profitable parts of the group under a new entity (the private workout); secured creditors were paid in full, and unprofitable units went into a new trust to be liquidated. The PUFG private workout maximised the group's best assets. In 581 days from the date of initial default, the court's approval was reached. The hybrid procedure allowed a state-link group to be saved.

However, these forms of private agreement and workouts are not without critiques. Think of the UK, where the hybrid model implemented through schemes of arrangement does not provide a moratorium and has high thresholds for the required approval from creditors to the plan. On the other hand, the advantages of schemes of arrangement are centred on assuring that secured and unsecured creditors are bound to the plan, and the stigma of insolvency is avoided because schemes of arrangement are disciplined under the Company Act 2006 (UK).

In a private workout, creditors and debtors negotiate the conditions of the debt's settlement and agree on the best possible solution in order to satisfy all parties. However, conflicts of interest are frequent between the parties at stake in insolvency scenarios, and agreements are hard to reach. Indeed, those agreements usually require unanimity among creditors. This unanimity is almost impossible to gather in practice as creditors' interests are various. According to Wood,[68] many workouts only involve banks without including the whole body of creditors. Indeed, a bank is keener to offer delays in payment rather than trade creditors who can have working capital requirements that call for quicker reimbursements. If unanimity is not reached, then it is very likely that the negotiation does not arrange the insolvent company's situation and may end in losing precious time and eventually lead to liquidation. The negotiation and settlement of a private workout will also be more complex as the number of creditors increases. Furthermore, these agreements are not approved by courts and creditors are not protected from any subsequent judicial procedure or default by the debtor other than classical contract law remedies. In other words, those agreements do not offer any guarantee to the parties other than those offered by contract law, and, in the end, any unsatisfied party may file a lawsuit, which will eventually end up disclosing the financial difficulties of the insolvent company. Thus, they may be reluctant to enter into such workouts, which can appear in their eyes as a way of delaying an inevitable liquidation procedure that would be more protective of their interests if it was introduced at an earlier point. Therefore, private workouts appear as the best solution to rescue a company, but, at the same time, they are criticised for their absence of legal framework.

For these reasons, since the late 1990s and the beginning of the twenty-first century, legal systems across the world started to develop a hybrid solution in order to conciliate all parties' interests at stake. Pre-packaged reorganisations are characterised as hybrid mechanisms because although they are essentially judicial reorganisations, court involvement is much more limited. It is more like a private negotiation that receives a seal of approval from the court, making the arrangement

---

68 Philip R Wood, *Principles of International Insolvency* (Sweet & Maxwell 2019).

legally binding. Furthermore, pre-pack confirmations can be achieved very quickly. For example, Sungard's Chapter 11 pre-packaged reorganisation plan was approved in 19 hours – a record for the United States.[69] This means that there is much less risk of stigma and related commercial impacts because by the time suppliers and customers are made aware there has been a restructuring, it will be completed and the company will no longer be in financial difficulty.

Summing up, traditionally, court-supervised procedures are lengthy, and demand detailed financial and commercial disclosure of information about the company. They can be expensive and can affect companies due to the stigma and bad reputation that is implied in disclosing financial difficulties.[70] Whether a company is in default or not, an insolvency filing can affect the relationship with trade creditors and suppliers and can trigger contractual cross-default provisions. The procedure might be slow, and the time spent on completing a reorganisation can affect the state of affairs of the company. Since insolvency law frameworks in many countries offer a moratorium on enforcement, in some jurisdictions, the commencement of an insolvency proceeding can only delay the liquidation of the company. This can lead to the liquidation of the business, which is contrary to the original rescue aim.

On the other hand, out-of-court reorganisation procedures known as "private workouts" are a viable solution. A private workout is a contractual agreement between the parties where the only requirement is for a contract to be valid.

One main difference between court-supervised and out-of-court procedures is the binding element. In a court-supervised procedure, the debtor benefits from a court order that makes the restructuring binding on all creditors involved in the reorganisation, whether they have accepted the plan or not. On the other hand, in private workouts, if unanimity is not achieved, the debtor will end up with one or more holdout creditors that will either be paid in full while other creditors will have to accept the reorganisation or be at risk of being legitimately sued in a court of law for the original full face-value claim.

The Covid-19 crisis has given rise to the need and opportunity for states to strengthen their restructuring regimes to prepare for the impact of such a crisis. To this end, states have started to implement a third system of regulation that can be defined as hybrid. As we have seen, the emergence of this trend is focused on pre-insolvency or preventive restructuring procedures that aim to facilitate informal negotiations between the debtor and its creditors and minimise the role of the court and insolvency administrators. A hybrid alternative is minimally supervised by a court or other governmental or independent body. It is commonly referred to as an out-of-court reorganisation although it has a court supervision element. The most important feature of this hybrid process is the binding effect of a formal reorganisation and the speed, flexibility, and non-adverse publicity

---

69 Wood, "Comparison of workouts, judicial rescues and liquidations" in *Principles of International Insolvency* (Sweet & Maxwell 2019).
70 Ibid, 33.

element of a private workout. This includes what is known as pre-packaged and pre-negotiated deals. Those tools are the direct evidence of the new role of the law that – as we said – tends to become de-centralised and more innovative and oriented towards practical solutions rather than abstract definitions and codifications. This is particularly evident if we examine a recent IMF Working Paper,[71] which analyses the breadth of choices of the Restructuring Directive. The Directive offers 143 different options of implementation. For example, some countries may choose to implement the Directive in a single stand-alone restructuring procedure or in two or more restructuring procedures (e.g. one for financial claims, and another more general and public restructuring mechanism). Since the hybrid restructuring procedure incorporates many elements of a formal reorganisation procedure, some countries may be even tempted to replace reorganisation with the new restructuring procedure, thereby eliminating reorganisation entirely. Those choices give rise to a new role for comparative law as a means of providing immediate and effective tools to debtors to facilitate their economic rescue. In other words, not only is the private and public divide that we have previously examined irremediably modified and changed with the absence of a central planner of the system, but the same role of comparative law tends to be transformed in looking at the law on the basis of its efficiency rather than quality. To this end, indicators become the evaluation tool in terms of measuring the efficiency of the law (see Chapter 4).

1.4 Comparative Law as a Policymaking Instrument of "Out-of-Law" Meanings

As can be seen in the numerous examples earlier, corporate and cross-border insolvency requires a hybrid restructuring procedure and usually starts from a private agreement among parties (the private workout); usually, it does not relate directly to the dominion of public law in the form of state law but rather gives rise to the central role of private autonomy and private law. The binding force of the private workout and therefore its enforceability however depend on the ratification of a judicial body that represents the court-supervised element. This can confirm our initial intuition based on the conviction that the law is not the input of the code but rather the output, through which the law confers a binding effect on the "out-of-law" compound. In other words, the codification process or, in Pistor's terms, the Code of Capital, has been broken; it has been permanently altered in a post-pandemic world. The role of law has dramatically changed, and the preventive restructuring procedures are some of the many pieces of evidence in international insolvency law and finance law. Indeed, under the Whereas n. 15 of the Restructuring Directive, it is stated:

---

71 IMF, "The IMF Working Paper: Restructuring and insolvency in Europe: Policy options in the implementation of the EU Directive" (May 2021) WP 152.

The differences between Member States which hamper the early restructuring of viable debtors in financial difficulties and the possibility of a discharge of debt for honest entrepreneurs should be reduced. Reducing such differences should bring greater transparency, legal certainty, and predictability across the Union. (…) Greater coherence of restructuring and insolvency procedure should also facilitate the restructuring of groups of companies irrespective of where the members of the group are located in the Union.

The law is becoming ever more focused on harmonisation processes to be decided at international level, and to this end, the role of comparative law is maximised. Comparative law becomes a useful tool to discover not only similarities and differences between legal systems at national level to facilitate harmonisation but especially also to analyse "non-legal" or "out-of-law" meanings that can effectively promote a coherent system of laws between countries. For example, the word "rescue" is not strictly speaking a "legal" word. In general terms, it means to save somebody or something from a dangerous or harmful situation. Several times this word appears in the Restructuring Directive, referring to business rescue and economic rescue. This is the main aim of preventive procedures, namely, to promote the rescue of economically viable debtors as well as discharge procedures for entrepreneurs and other natural persons – to save viable businesses from liquidation.

The new codification process of a post-pandemic world necessarily starts from the inclusion in the law of "non-legal" meanings and from the harmonisation of the law via "non-legal" meanings, such as rescue, sustainability in terms of corporate objectives, and sovereign debt of emerging countries. Those are instances of what I define and discuss further in Chapter 2 as examples of (legal) constants. To implement the new Code of Capital, comparative law is using assessment reports, and it is evaluating national law frameworks on the basis of efficiency rather than quality, and countries' ability to reform the law against specific benchmarks that are established at the international level. Indicators serve the role of facilitating such assessments and evaluating a country's own legislative framework against established international standards that will be further discussed in Chapter 4 of this work.

1.5 Conclusions

In this chapter, we have analysed the LTF of Pistor, and her evolving theory of the "Code of Capital". The main findings have brought us to challenge and question her view of the world, according to which the law is code. Law is no more the "input" of any possible codification process, but rather the output, namely, the means through which private agreements and non-legal concepts are rendered "legal". This gives rise to a new concept of comparative law that can be identified for the first time as (legal) constant.

Enforceability is still a key concept of any legal system, but the mode or process through which enforceability is guaranteed is not necessarily related to a conception of hard law as promulgated by the state, or rather as a concept that is pertinent to the law more broadly.

Private agreements, soft law, and self-regulation practices can effectively provide the system with the same degree of efficiency that hard law or codification processes have aimed to achieve for centuries in a pre-pandemic world. The virus has not only had a major impact on health; it has changed our *modus operandi*, and our minds forever. As opposed to Pistor, finance is not legally construed. Finance does stand outside the law. However, Pistor had the merit to identify how contract law plays a major role in financial markets. Nonetheless, market participants and financial operators are no longer obliged or compelled to follow pre-established standards (the 143 options of implementation of the Restructuring Directive are a direct instance of this new approach). Financial markets are fluid, and market practices can create new financial innovations. This is because uncertainty is not synonymous with a crisis in the shortage of liquidity of assets, as Pistor would like to assert. By contrast, uncertainty has a prominent role in the new financial architecture, promoting competition among parties and sustaining financial innovations as catalysts of market regeneration. Furthermore, it is the uncertainty of the financial crisis that is indirectly providing access to new finance in business reorganisations. For example, new financing is frequently protected by national insolvency frameworks, or, at least, the protection of new financing is an important feature of any modernised insolvency, together with other key elements, such as the moratorium. This is because the new rescue culture – as we said – is becoming prominent in insolvency practices that are always more focused on hybrid restructuring procedures where the role of private law and private autonomy is maximised. This would have never been possible without the remarkable and transforming role of uncertainty (see Chapter 3).

Contract law is not only playing a vital role in the insolvency practices of business reorganisations. It is a driving force to create exceptions to established legal principles such as *pari passu*. It is not by chance that this same principle is not defined in any legal instrument or legal provision. Law is not the input. Although many times we might find a definition of the *pari passu* principle in private law, namely, contractual arrangements such as sovereign debt instruments (bond prospectus or the offering memorandum or circular). Those same definitions are not legally binding to other debt instruments, and they are not of general application.

This shows that the law is rarely the "input", but often the "output", especially in a post-pandemic world. Flexibility is key, and to deal with financial innovations such as those we experience in the Fintech area or de-centralised finance, we must find common meanings that can be subsequently codified as legal constants. Non-legal meanings are "diversity", "environment", "network", "payment", "rescue", "sustainability", "virtual", and so on. They all have a meaning beyond the law. Those non-legal meanings are then many times recognised by soft law instruments, and therefore, non-binding instruments beyond a hard law conception of the law. The extent of enforceability of these new legal constants will then depend on the level of cooperation and agreement to be found among international non-state actors (ICMA, ISDA, World Bank Group [WBG], IMF, etc.) and national governments. This is the new apex of contemporary financial markets, and it is here that the new role of the law is unfolding. A very good example of this phenomenon are the new guidelines released in October 2021 by the Financial Action Task Force (*i.e.* an international body that coordinates government policy on illicit finance) to force cryptocurrency firms to take greater steps to combat money laundering. The task force called on governments to broaden regulatory oversight of crypto firms and forced more of them to take measures such as checking the identities of customers or reporting suspicious transactions to regulators. It is important to highlight that those guidelines do not have the force of law, and need to be implemented by national regulators in each country. However, the task force is influential in setting standards for government policies against money laundering and financing terrorism, and its guidelines could shape new crypto regulations. Indeed, this example can show how an international organisation is able to influence national hard legislations and in so doing we might assert that is hardening soft law. The key point is that guiding principles established in a soft law instrument are making those constants harder by virtue of national hard laws in an undeniable debacle of national governments that are no more in charge unless they follow the international standards mutually agreed by international organisations at the international level.

In the following chapters, we will further explain the theory of (legal) constant(s) (Chapter 2). Chapter 3 will provide the theoretical background to risk and uncertainty in financial markets. Specifically, the role of uncertainty is examined from an ontological and epistemological point of view in order to establish how this changing force is not only modifying the thinking of the businessperson or investor of today but especially the level of regulation that states are able to put in place in an effort to counterbalance it. Uncertainty-aversion paradigms will be revealed and criticised for their lack of understanding of uncertainty as a catalyst for profit. The role of competition is re-examined as a force that is making financing opportunities available to private parties. Risk, uncertainty, competition, and financial innovation: these are the four main structures of financial systems. The theoretical background built up in Chapters 1, 2, and 3 serves the appreciation of the practical examples of legal constants as well as risk and uncertainty in contemporary financial markets that are provided in Chapter 4. In this chapter, we have also introduced the role of insolvency law assessments, and how those evaluations are making comparative law an essential policy instrument to promote a new harmonisation of the law and discover non-legal meanings that might become further legal constants at international level, and subsequently in the domestic environment through the implementation phase at national level. Consolidating remarks are provided in the Conclusions.

2   Legal Constants, and the Constant Outside of the Law

2.1 Theories of Comparative Law: The Law as "Input"

There are a number of views on how to define comparative law, but the purpose of this work is to provide a literature review. However, some key concepts will be highlighted in relation to comparative law in order to introduce here, for the first time, the concept of legal constants, and to reflect on how the application of legal constants might benefit the law and legal systems, especially at times of crisis.

According to Zweigert and Kötz, comparative law is "the comparison of different legal systems of the World".[1] In Bogden's view, however, comparative law is about comparing different legal systems to ascertain their similarities and differences, and by working with these, ultimately identifying the common core of legal systems. A similar approach to comparative law was introduced by Rodolfo Sacco, who first theorised legal formants.[2] If indeed we examine the legal world through the lens of legal formants, we are surely right to define comparative law as a science that increases our knowledge. Sacco highlights, furthermore, that knowledge is only one function of comparative law; its main function is to discover similarities and differences among legal systems and allow jurists to borrow – in the term accepted by Watson[3] – legal institutions into their own legal system. This is what Sacco defines as the principal aim of comparative law; legal formants really represent an instrument for jurists to influence and change their own domestic systems.

Comparative law in this light is seen as a rebellious tool to influence the law dynamically. However, what is missing in the Sacco analysis is an understanding of comparative law beyond its functions, namely conceptualising comparative law as the study of different legal meanings rather than different legal systems. I shall argue that borrowing legal institutions can never achieve a perfect "transplant". In other words, once we include a borrowed legal institution in our own domestic system, we are essentially borrowing a legal meaning that was once

---

1 Zweigert and Kotz, *An Introduction to Comparative Law* (3rd edn, Oxford University Press 2008) 2.
2 Rodolfo Sacco, "Legal formants: A dynamic approach to comparative law" (1991) 39 American Journal of Comparative Law 1.
3 Alan Watson, "Aspects of reception of law" (1996) 44 American Journal of Comparative Law 335.

DOI: 10.4324/9781003278320-3

"transplanted" from or implemented inside another legal system, and it is influenced by other legal meanings. The final outcome can therefore never resemble the initial legal meaning that we borrowed. The 143 options of implementation of the Restructuring Directive that we mentioned in Chapter 1 is a self-evident example because the actual operation of preventive restructuring tools depends on the national legal frameworks of each EU member state, and sometimes full implementation can even be difficult because of possible conflicts with national legal principles that tend to favour the position of secured creditors and limit the full operation of private workouts.

This is at least the conception of legal transplants we are used to thinking about. There is an evolved form of legal transplant that is often found today in cooperation mechanisms activated at international level where principles of law, or sometimes even non-legal best practices, are established in order to then be received by national legal orders (see, for practical instances, Chapter 4). I define those instances as legal constants because they are based on shared meanings that are mainly formed out of the law.

In addition to insolvency law (see Chapters 1 and 4), another area where we can experience the direct relevance of legal constants is financial technology, or Fintech. Here, there are no legal definitions for the new legal institutions such as mobile payments, the blockchain, smart contracts, and so on. These are technical innovations that have seen rapid growth, and the emergence of new types of payment services in the marketplace imposes a necessary rethinking of the need to regulate electronic money devices. For this reason, mobile payments and blockchain are generally subject to the principle of technical neutrality, through which technological developments must not be subject to strict regulation, although they must be provided with legal status and certainty must not occur in a possible legal vacuum. The principle of technical neutrality is one of the leading principles of the EU law of payment services, so the de-centralised infrastructure of blockchain is not contemplated in the new legislative framework. This is because the revised Payment Service Directive (namely, the so-called PSD2) only provides a centralised infrastructure of the provisions of payment services. Therefore, every time, every single domestic system is capable of attributing different legal meanings or definitions to mobile payments, smart contracts, or blockchain, depending on what the legal system aims to protect – the consumer, competition between firms, and so on. In other words, a specific definition is adopted in consideration of the aims or values, or better, non-legal meanings, that the legal system seeks to protect. This way of qualifying facts under the paradigm of the law is quite natural in law studies. However, the main question still goes unanswered today; namely, is there a common meaning that can be unanimously legally recognised by regulators, judges, scholars, and lawmakers by which a legal constant can be identified? It is important, therefore, to focus our attention on the concept of legal constants that are based on out-of-law meanings and on a conception of the law as "output".

Pistor, Sacco, and others conceptualise a theory of comparative law based on one principal input: the law itself. In Pistor's view, the law and its enforcement are tools to protect parties' interests, mainly with the objective of hedging the strongest party. In her conception of the code of capital, legal formants have always been used to discretionally protect specific interests, such as the segregation of assets through the concept of corporate legal personality, or the vindication of land from aborigines. In her view, to compare different laws means to compare different codes in order to identify a global code of capital that ultimately translates into a sort of universal codification that can apply to different legal systems and different legal traditions: a sort of "colonisation" of the law within Western terms. This is not only a political view of comparative law but also a limited one if we think about the latest unfolding pandemic crisis where the role of law has been dramatically changed and traditional law paradigms have had to be abandoned and replaced by a new non-legal conception of the law as "output" rather than "input".

2.1.1 The Functions and Aims of Comparative Law

Comparative law is deputed to find a common substrate in the development of different legal systems, although it could be argued that simply identifying the common core or substrate is not enough where a function and aim for comparison is lacking. With increasing knowledge being identified as one of the key aims of comparative law, other key aims and functions include supporting the construction and reconstruction of a legal system,[4] making it easier for judges to interpret existing domestic laws, legal education, and international unification of laws.

One of the most important aims of comparative law is the harmonisation process that the study and comparison of different laws can sustain and promote. To this end, even an EU directive or regulation can be seen as a practical and direct instance of such a harmonisation process. Nonetheless, the numerous aims and functions of comparative law are unable to describe or grasp its intimate essence, which rests upon an understanding of what I define as legal constants. This new research approach of studying legal systems by virtue of legal constants entails the analysis of legal systems through a common substrate that is capable of discovering what can be defined as legal constants that are the result of interpretation and construction of different legal meanings attributed to different legal institutions (*i.e.* laws, principles, and jurisprudence) or sometimes even to non-legal words, such as rescue and sustainability. Merely observing and describing legal institutions makes no sense without interpreting them.

Hence, meaning is the ultimate objective of a legal analysis in comparative law, as well as in any interpretative activity in national or domestic systems (*i.e.* interpretation is the core activity that judges carry out in every legal system in order to solve a dispute; and interpretation is the main legal activity of lawyers, who defend their clients by providing judges with a different qualification of the facts). It is misleading to see comparative law as the comparison of different legal

---

4 Basil Markesinis, *Foreign Law and Comparative Methodology: A Subject and Thesis* (Hart Publishing 1997).

systems because actually, the main aim of the comparison relates to the study of different legal meanings, by which different legal constants can be discovered.

2.1.2 Comparative Law as a Tool for Studying (Legal) Meanings

Beyond the functions and aims of comparative law, it is crucial to find a common substrate in the development of different legal systems, as well as in the comparison activity itself, in order to study the differences and similarities among legal systems under a common kaleidoscope, namely the activity of interpretation.

According to this approach, comparative law does not simply refer to the comparison of different legal systems, because this is only a descriptive function of comparative law. It is a function that directly relates to the activity of stating the law, such as in legal opinions when lawyers describe and illustrate the law of their domestic systems to their clients. However, it is in the application of the law to the facts that both lawyers and judges are compelled to interpret the law by giving the legal provisions a particular meaning. It is indeed by virtue of such meaning that the facts are interpreted, qualified, and categorised through different laws or decisions depending on the legal system that we are examining, such as that of civil law or common law countries.

From this point, we can start understanding that comparative law is, indeed, the science of comparison of different legal systems, but the real subject matter of the comparison is different legal meanings that judges, lawyers, and scholars attribute to different legal provisions or decisions by virtue of a unique activity: interpretation. I shall argue that this approach to comparative law is not totally new because as we said before, Rodolfo Sacco was famously one of the first to theorise legal formants as tools for interpreting different legal systems. Nonetheless, both the analyses provided by Sacco and Pistor lack an understanding of the law based on non-legal instances. This is because those theorisations of comparative law strictly conceptualise the law as "input". In the end, this is the role of any codification process, namely, to codify natural and human facts by virtue of the law. Without the law, those same natural or human facts would never be able to have legal effects. It is, indeed, a conception of the law that rests upon a positivist approach, once theorised by Hans Kelsen, which does not reflect the complexities imposed by new emerging paradigms, accelerated by the appearance of Covid-19 and dictated more generally by the infinite cycle determined by financial crises.

2.2 Legal Constant(s)

A legal constant cannot be construed only as a common element that can be discovered while studying different legal systems. Indeed, the concept of a legal constant is based not just on the idea that a legal institution is present in two or more legal systems, but on the fact that a legal constant is the constant meaning derived from the interpretation of different legal institutions, and it is usually identified as the only meaning that can relate to and justify the comparison between two or more different laws, two or more different principles, or two or more judgements:

it is not just a common element, because a common element has only a descriptive function.

A legal constant is more easily identified when the borrowing activity of legal institutions occurs in a domestic system. This is because identifying a constant legal meaning makes it easier to apply a borrowed legal institution within a domestic system.

A legal constant is the result of the interpretation and construction of different meanings that are derived from a legal system, or more precisely, from the comparison of two or more legal systems as well as two or more decisions. Specifically, the interpreter is focused on finding a constant outside of the law to which regulators, judges, lawyers, scholars, and lawmakers give a legal meaning so that we speak of legal constants where the "legal" qualification is only a subsequent identification of a non-legal concept that is recognised as a common meaning for one or more legal systems, as well as one or more decisions.

Meaning is the ultimate objective of legal analysis in comparative law, as well as within any national or domestic system (for instance, interpretation is the core activity that judges carry out in every legal system to solve a dispute; or interpretation is the main legal activity of lawyers who defend their clients by providing judges with a different qualification of the facts and/or provisions). For this reason, the idea that comparative law is the comparison of different legal systems is misleading because, essentially, the main comparison being carried out is directly related to the study of different meanings, by which different legal constants can be discovered through the examination of either legal transplants or legal formants. In view of this, legal transplants and legal formants represent "working tools" for the interpreter to first identify a constant meaning outside of the law.

2.2.1 The Constant(s) Outside of the Law and Legal Constant(s)

A legal constant cannot be construed only as a common element to be discovered while studying different legal systems. Indeed, the concept of a legal constant is not simply based on the idea that a legal institution exists in two or more legal systems,[5] but on the fact that a legal constant is the constant legal meaning derived

---

5 For instance, the right of one party to terminate a contract is a right that is usually present in many different legal systems, namely under English Common law as well as Civil law countries such as Italy, France, Germany, and so on, but the mere fact that this element exists in more than one country does not make it a legal constant. In light of this, it can be considered only a simple common element that has mainly a descriptive function; to provide the reader with another example: divorce exists in more than one legal system such as under English Common law, Civil law countries, and in some cases also under Islamic law. The termination in contract law as well as divorce in family law are considered in this instance as a common element of the law that is present and exists in one or more legal systems, but it is not a legal constant. Indeed, a legal constant can be appreciated in the research of a common legal meaning that is mainly identified by a constant meaning outside of the law to which jurists, judges, scholars, and lawmakers give legal status. For instance, in mobile payments we find a constant meaning outside of law that mobile payments deeply relate to, and such process qualifies the legal recognition of this constant meaning outside of the law as a legal constant

from the interpretation of different legal institutions, and it is usually identified as the only meaning that can relate to and justify the comparison between two or more different laws, two or more different principles, or two or more judgements.

A legal constant is not just a common element, because a common element has itself only a descriptive function and can identify only the objective existence of a legal institution in one or more legal systems, although subject to different interpretations and meanings. For this reason, the interpreter whose objective is to find a legal constant must first identify a constant meaning outside of the law that is derived from the comparison of two or more legal systems or judgements and is then given a legal qualification that consequently allows it to be identified as a legal constant. In other words, although the interpretation of different laws enacted in different legal systems can equate to different legal meanings, a legal constant is the only meaning capable of unifying all those different meanings under a common one. It is a unique form of interpretation to read laws, principles, and case law that have been enacted, developed, and upheld in different countries, at different times, and by different interpreters.

I shall also highlight how a meaning outside of the law indirectly detaches that same concept from the law so that the main field of application of this alienation of meanings can be easily identified for instance in commercial concepts (such as payment, business customs, risk management, etc.) or concepts related to the private sphere such as intimacy, dignity, privacy, marriage, and equality. Essentially, every concept that is capable of multiple definitions in different fields of inquiry, or different subjects such as economics, biology, anthropology, and philosophy can be identified subsequently as legal constants where the interpreter is able to find a possible legal meaning that is attributed to such a concept. This is why we speak about legal constants as common meanings that are identified in different legal formants such as statutory laws and judgements. Those formants once interpreted convey the same meaning; they identify a legal constant that can be used later to provide definitions for legal institutions and to outline the intimate function of that concept in order to provide more protection for consumers, customers, and private parties (for instance, the non-legal word "family" is a direct instance where the private interests of children – a concept outside of the law based on love and affection – must be protected against the "egoistic" interests of adults mainly based on economic interests. Here, for example, the same concept of "maintenance" can constitute a legal constant of many family law institutions, such as divorce, separation, adoption, marriage, and abortion). Legal constants are based on a constant outside of the law because only beyond the law is the interpreter free to identify the intimate meaning of every legal institution. Furthermore, being the law indirectly conceived as a political tool, it necessarily follows that tolerance of different races,

---

(in this specific case, for example, the payment function is seen as a constant outside of the law to which European legislation as well as judgements of the European Commission grant legal status to protect several public interests such as consumer protection and technological network safety).

cultures, and religions can only occur in a neutral space beyond the law appositely created in a common out-of-law meaning or constant. In other words, we must first think (un)legally to become legal. This is because our humanity is based on non-legal concepts and law relates to humans, hence, to find the intimate essence of every law, we have to re-start our discourse from the human being and from his/her needs.

2.2.2 The Development of Legal Constants in Commercial Law

One field of law where the importance of legal constants may be most appreciated is commercial law. This book has examined in depth one of the most important areas of commercial law; that is, insolvency law. This is because the evolution in insolvency law practices that we outlined in Chapter 1 provides us with direct evidence that the role of law, the courts, and judicial enforcement have been marginalised in preventive restructuring. Today, to put in place preventive restructuring mechanisms means to primarily rely on private workouts and out-of-court agreements. This has necessarily increased the role of contract law and contractarian theories, according to which the resolution of viable businesses must be initiated by negotiation and a creditor-bargain approach. Following agreements, the courts play a minimal role and are only called to ratify the contents of those agreements that can also become binding on dissenting minorities. The hybrid nature of those pre-packaged mechanisms is also a symptom of an increased role for non-legal solutions and out-of-law meanings that incentivise a spontaneous *motus* of compliance rather than an imposed decision deriving from a strict application of the law by courts. There is no rigid scheme to be followed and no need for a central planner for insolvency law procedures. Paradoxically, insolvency law is losing both its insolvency nature and its legal quality and is being replaced by less rigid remedies disciplined by company or contract law and out-of-law meanings. The non-legal word "rescue" that we find in the Restructuring Directive associated with business rescue is a direct example of an out-of-law meaning to which the European Union institutions have attributed the meaning of business rescue. This latter is a legal constant that a hard law instance (the directive) has recognised as the common and unified meaning among member states to save viable distressed businesses. How such business rescue will operate is subject to specific contents that each member state will each time decide to follow discretionally and implement in its insolvency law framework. Once again the 143 implementation options of the Restructuring Directive means that today the order in insolvency, as well as in other law areas, is not always connected to the global level, and the local level must provide answers that are tailored to its legal principles. Although the implementation of legal constants can be particular and specific (the local level), the establishment of every legal constant mainly occurs at the international level by virtue of cooperation between and among states. In other words, the local level will be inspired by contents that are decided at the apex: the international sphere.

Another example in commercial law that is particularly important for its application effects is the principle of good faith. The latter is controversial and there is a lack of comparative studies on this topic.[6] The concept is very broad and is not recognised by every legal system in Europe, although the majority take this into account due to common Roman law origins. Although the principle of good faith has different meanings under contract law and in commercial dealings, I argued in 2018[7] how it could be possible to establish an original meaning of good faith that is unaltered. The principle of good faith had a remarkable story under Roman law. It started as a public conception of trust that was strongly connected to the sacredness of *fas* (in ancient Latin, the religious sphere). A private and objective conception of *bona fides* (good faith) becomes, in the modern age, a legally binding principle to be observed during the life of private transactions. The latter meaning, informed by a principle of universality, led to the modern creation of the *lex mercatoria,* which was a product of the decisions of the international arbiter. The principle of good faith dominated international private transactions in the modern age, but at the same time, *lex mercatoria* evolved, with a system of harmonising rules such as the UNIDROIT Principles of International Commercial Contracts (UPICC), the Principles of European Contract Law (PECL), the Common Frame of Reference (CFR), legislative acts (the withdrawn EU Proposal for a Common European Sales Law), and a Treaty (the United Nations Convention on Contracts for the International Sale of Goods, known as CISG). They recognised the private dimension of good faith, sometimes as a general clause and at other times as a general principle. The majority of these Acts, apart from the CISG, have either a soft law or non-binding nature (*i.e.* UPICC, PECL, CFR).

Good faith is yet another direct example of a legal constant; quasi-legal instruments or hard law acts such as the CISG treaty recognised a common and unified meaning of good faith that can then be applied and implemented in different national legislative frameworks. Since then, good faith has mainly been interpreted as a general clause rather than a general principle. However, the peculiarity of good faith is that it can be considered both as a general principle and a general clause. It is a general principle because it is the *genus* on which professional diligence, the information duties *in contrahendo* and the abuse of rights are specifications; it is a general clause because it represents a consolidated standard of conduct within a specific social context where the conduct of the contractual party takes place. The etymology of good faith can further confirm this interpretation. The Latin term *fides* can reveal different meanings in the English language such as "faith, belief, confidence, reliance, belief without evidence or proof, and belief based on testimony or authority".[8] As a result, the open-ended meaning of *fides* can show a main understanding of the word in terms of trust, faith, and belief,

6 Reinhard Zimmermann, Simon Whittaker, Mauro Bussani, *Good Faith in European Contract Law* (Cambridge University Press 2000).

7 Daniele D'Alvia, "From public law to private law: The remarkable story of *bona fides*" in Maren Heidemann and Joseph Lee (eds) *The Future of the Commercial Contract in Scholarship and Law Reform* (Springer 2018).

8 Lesley Brown, *The New Shorter Oxford English Dictionary on Historical Principles* (Clarendon Press 1993).

namely all terms that are intimately connected to a religious character or dimension. *Fides* is primarily an ethical concept, to which the law attributes a juridical and legal meaning that can also be reflected in the production of legal effects, such as in the case of adverse possession. Indeed, here transfer of ownership or the achievement of profit must be made available only to a faithful possessor who has to act in good faith at the moment he or she acquires the possession of a specific item, albeit *mala fides* can supervene at a later stage. This latter circumstance does not have any legal effect and cannot prejudice the final transfer of ownership, because the main concern is to guarantee that at the start of possession, the possessor does not prejudice the interests of any third party. In this sense, it is possible to appreciate what can be defined as an ethical dimension of *fides* in the form of moral respect for other private parties.

In light of this, accepting good faith as a general clause imposes on the contractual parties a duty to act in good faith. It is a standard social clause by which the judge is invited to evaluate and assess the conduct of private parties in the course of their affairs. General clauses are provisions that are drafted in the form of open textured terms, and they refer to a consolidated standard of conduct or model, as well as shared evaluations of a social context from which the judge by virtue of interpretation creates the specific rule that determines the dispute.

This is a private approach to good faith in the sense that there is a standardisation of good faith into a clause that serves as a parameter for the judicial application of social justice. Again, particular and local answers are provided to established and general meanings that in the case of the evolution of good faith have mainly been established at international level. This example also shows the point that I have previously fixed in theory, namely that the identification of a common or unified meaning or constant must necessarily be derived from an interpretation activity. This is a dynamic evolution of the law, and it can eventually provide strong evidence for how comparative law is construed as the science of knowledge of studying different legal meanings rather than different legal systems. Finally good faith, in terms of general clause and general principle, is based on a non-legal word, faith, and on a non-legal origin of the term which, as we have explained, was derived from Roman law under a public vision of trust within the religious sphere, and therefore, the moral understanding of the term is of religious faith.

2.3 The Uncodified-Codification of the Law

For Sacco, legal formants are "descriptors" of the law. To compare different legal systems, the law must be construed as the output of three distinct legal formants, namely statute law, legal scholarship, and judicial decisions. This means that common law jurisdictions are based on a prevalent judicial legal formant rather than on statute law, and civil law traditions are based on the opposite approach. Building on this theory, I have explained the new legal arguments on the assumption that the law is based on dynamic creation processes rather than descriptive ones, and it represents the output and not the initial input of any law creation process. It means that to compare different legal systems does not necessarily mean to compare different laws or judicial decisions. This is only a descriptive feature of comparative law. To this end, Sacco's approach looks at the "codified" process of comparative law rather than starting with its "uncodified" or out-of-law meanings. For this reason, Pistor's theory of the "Code of Capital" is exposed. She argues that capital has been codified for centuries by means of the law. In her view, "Law is Code". Hence, codification becomes the main instrument through which power and private interests can be protected. This is an inappropriate conception of comparative law that cannot properly address the new challenges of a pre- and post-Covid-19 legal environment. To this end, Covid-19 has only been an accelerator rather than an initiator of non-legal instances of codification.

2.3.1 The Uncodified Law and Crisis

This book has focused on a new role that comparative law can play in financial crises and the Covid-19 pandemic based on the "uncodified" processes of the law. It seems that Pistor's theory can be turned on its head. In other words, today, the law is "dead" and is not the starting point of our discourse.

Once constants or common meanings are identified, they are used to promote the creation of harmonisation processes through which the law can subsequently identify a common legal meaning to be codified in domestic legislation. This is what I define as the "uncodified-codification" of the law. Essentially, common international features in different areas of commercial law, from insolvency law to payment services, before the inception of legal principles such as the one we explained in good faith, were recognised by virtue of the reception or codification of uncodified common meanings as international standards or best practices to be followed.

As a result, the law is not the input to codify the capital, but rather the output that is the result of an identification and recognition of constant meaning(s) outside of the law. Hence, our approach to legal codifications is irremediably changed. By comparing different laws, we are not comparing them in the search for highlighting commonalities and differences and identifying a global code by virtue of "exporting the law". This is still a simplistic comparison of laws, and it is based on an old conception of legal transplants. It is descriptive rather than dynamic. By contrast, comparative law must be re-invented and re-interpreted to study different meanings that are mainly to be found outside of the law.

2.4 Conclusions

This chapter has briefly outlined a new theory in comparative law and has labelled it as (legal) constants. Basically, in mathematical terms, this is a negative expression where the inputs, the constants, are always outside of the law and only become legal once they are identified and recognised throughout legal systems.

First, the establishment of a constant as a common meaning is created at international level by virtue of quasi-legal frameworks based mainly on a direct soft law approach, although hard law at international level can still be a possibility (see the Restructuring Directive). What really matters here is the cooperation mechanism among States and international organisations at international (*i.e.* the new apex) rather than national level. In this chapter, we have examined examples of this process in commercial law practices with a particular focus on the principle of good faith and business rescue under the new preventive restructuring culture. Those practical instances are further explained in Chapter 4 because they probably represent the best examples to demonstrate the (legal) constant theory and its influence on future developments of the law.

We have claimed that the law is "dead". The French Revolution was directed primarily against private oppression (the remnants of the feudal system and the power and privilege of the Church and aristocracy) and the judicial class that was its bulwark. On the other hand, the American Revolution was perceived as a rebellion against the abuse of public power (the British government and colonial authorities). In both instances, the law plays a central role. The documents embodying the revolutionary programmes and expressing the deepest aspirations of each society necessarily took different forms: a constitution in the United States and a code of private law in France. The time of the French and American Revolutions has passed.

The modern state has progressively been substituted by non-state authorities that sit at international level (IMF, WBG, ICMA, ISDA, etc.) There is no further need for a central planner, and the law does not necessarily have to be interpreted by the judges, but rather by policymakers and technicians. This is why the role of comparative law today is maximised as a tool to inform policy decisions based on law assessments and reports that are conducted at international level by the same international organisations that are deputed to identify common meanings or constants. The law is no longer seen as a rebellious tool against oppression. The period of declarations of human rights after the Second World War followed the same pattern. Today, the role of law has dramatically changed and this shift in approach has contributed to an inversion of the traditional duality law-code.

This strong statement has become the starting point of a new epistemological discourse on the law. In light of this, we can confidently say that today the knowledge of the law is the knowledge of common and unified non-legal meanings; these are better defined as constants. This means that an epistemological discourse on the law necessarily starts from a non-legal instance that is pertinent to the reign of the "uncodified". Subsequently, because the main role of the law is to codify private interests and qualify conducts and behaviours – essentially facts – with a legal effect, the law renders those out-of-law meanings as legal. This is the uncodified-codification of the law, and it is the new compelling process through which contemporary national legislations are modified. Generally, the national level follows the international one and to this end the European Union project is self-explanatory, but the same can be said for other international organisations (IMF, WBG, ICMA, ISDA, etc.) that through their quasi-legal frameworks are now able to inform political decisions at national level, as well as reforming the law. In other words, the law is no longer enacted as a form of reaction against oppression, but it is modelled on cooperation systems beyond national borders.

This new approach is not just a result of the globalisation process that occurred after the liberalisation of financial markets when investment banks started to engage in managing financial risk through cross-border transactions; this phenomenon is the direct result of an evolved form of capitalism where the role of uncertainty in financial markets has paved the way to a new financial architecture. It is the focus of the next chapter to further delve into this concept and explain how the role of the law in contemporary financial markets is strictly connected to the new structures of the market: risk, uncertainty, competition, and financial innovation.

3 The Un(codified) Financial Systems in Times of Crisis

3.1 The Ontology of Risk

Our lives are often affected by unexpected events, from natural disasters such as hurricanes and tornadoes to pandemics and financial crises. Some represent external shocks, such as pandemics or natural events, and others are simply internal failures of the system, such as the collapse of Lehman Brothers in 2008 (see Chapter 1). In other words, risk is everywhere and anywhere, especially in financial markets. The attempt to define financial risk has become a compelling need for the financial industry since the inception of systemic risk with the GFC (2007–2010).

To define risk in ontological terms is complex. This is because the story of risk has always been a story of rebellion. "Better to reign in Hell, than to serve in Heaven" is John Milton's famous sentence in Paradise Lost, written in blank verse in 1667. The figurative image of the Devil here represents the story of human beings who are struggling to take control of their destiny in a new era where progress is determined by individual choices, and it is connected to the very idea of taking risks and facing uncertainties, two separate and distinct activities, as this chapter seeks to explain.

To face uncertainty in the form of Hell, one must be prepared to manage risks in rational ways, at least from an actuarial perspective, under the laws of probability. For centuries, risk management has been a reliable method of generating reasonable incomes by virtue of insurance through risk isolation. Isolating risk is a classical insurance activity that validates the very existence of insurance itself. Insurance operates best when it successfully implements a distribution of risk based on the individual risk taken by each operator. This second stage requires a proper risk assessment, though a sophisticated assessment that is almost completely accurate is not feasible. The future can never be predicted with certainty. As a result, the distribution of risk by classification based on the expected loss can promote economic efficiency, despite the fact that risk assessment and its distribution can create an inevitable tension.[1] This is because when there is a poor

---

1 Kenneth S. Abraham, *Distributing Risk: Insurance, Legal Theory and Public Policy* (Yale University Press 1986) 64.

DOI: 10.4324/9781003278320-4

risk assessment and proper classification and isolation of risks are missed, then inefficient behaviours in terms of moral hazards may occur.

Risk and uncertainty are two main features of financial markets. They both characterise markets in terms of their intimate essence as venues that are capable of matching the opposite interests of lenders and borrowers and finding a perfect allocation of resources. Risk-aversion entities and risk-taker operators dominate markets and even our own lives. It is our approach to life that makes us risk-takers or risk-averse. Risk-takers are the most vibrant figures in what I define as the "human-humanity" paradigm of risk[2] through which human history has evolved over the centuries. Risk-taking is a form of progress and societal evolution. Hence, to study risk and uncertainty in their ontological meanings, it is essential to conceptualise uncertainty as something that cannot be controlled or governed, and the ontology of risk refers to its metaphysical status as a quality in the physical world. From an ontological point of view, the discourse on risk has manifested the objective nature of risk. It is not by chance that human beings tend to dominate the future, or better, in the words of Giddens,[3] to colonise it. It comes from a desire to expect, to predict, a risk-free world. From a historical point of view, this argument has been endorsed for centuries in Western countries, in Fibonacci's *Liber Abaci* (1202), Cardano's *Liber de Ludo Aleae* (1525), and Galileo's *Sopra la Scoperta dei dadi* (1623) through the laws of probability framed, *inter alia*, by Pascal and Fermat,[4] and in particular, the science of statistics of Graunt, Petty, and Halley,[5] promoting the concept of insurance as a commercial tool in the eighteenth century. In other words, the story of risk was initiated by formalising its ontological meaning (a theory of being) based on an objective dimension under the laws of probability.

Nonetheless, the discourse on risk is much more complex if its subjective dimension is taken into account and it is constructed as a value that varies according to the context. A risk-free world might be made theoretically possible by implementing highly restrictive policies that would often be likely to achieve unreasonable objectives. For instance, imagine a case of zero automobile fatalities; this might be possible, and any risk could be eradicated by outlawing motor vehicles. The same is true for drowning, which could be eradicated by outlawing swimming and bathing. These examples already tell us something about the irrationality of such restrictive and hard policies. It means that we cannot totally eradicate risk or live in a risk-free world, otherwise the same science of probability and statistics would have never been proved useful for measuring risk. Following the Black Death, the plague that is believed to have killed 60% of Europe's population in the second half of the fourteenth century, we have realised

2 Daniele D'Alvia, "Risk, uncertainty and the market: A rethinking of Islamic and Western finance" (2020) 16 (4) International Journal of Law in Context 339; Daniele D'Alvia, "L'umanità del rischio e l'ontologia dell'incertezza nei mercati finanziari" (2018) 17 IANUS 87.

3 Anthony Giddens, *Modernity and Self-Identity* (Stanford University Press 1991).

4 Peter L. Bernstein, *Against the Gods: The Remarkable Story of Risk* (Wiley 1998) 57–72.

5 Ibid, 92.

that life is short and full of risks. It was a historic disruption to everyday life, the likes of which we have not seen in most of our lifetimes.

Could we witness very long-term effects from the present contagion in Covid-19? Covid-19 is not as deadly as bubonic plague, and our tools to deal with pandemics today are far better stacked than when the pestilence reached the harbour of Messina on the north-eastern coast of Sicily in late 1347. However, our thinking to deal with pandemics is still highly influenced by our incapacity to deal with uncertainty. Since the outbreak of Covid-19 governments around the world have been trying to handle the pandemic. Governments have frequently offered their citizens the possibility of a zero-Covid world. This is as irrational as speaking of zero automobile fatalities or a zero-drowning world. Risk can be curtailed or measured, but it cannot be wholly eradicated. In other words, we must deal with uncertainty to sustain progress in our society. And yet New Zealand, Australia, and especially China have embraced zero-Covid policies. Those countries have imposed the most onerous lockdowns since Covid's inception in 2020, and they have imposed sharp restrictions on international travel, business closures, and so on. Nonetheless, once the restrictions were lifted and after the celebration of a zero-Covid world, the same virus came back in the form of the Delta variant in mid-2021. Since the inception of the Delta variant, many have indeed started to wonder whether this pandemic is permanent. This is because the Delta variant is more than twice as infectious as the virus humanity has been fighting since 2020. This variant seems to be able to evade even the best defences, which are the mRNA vaccines produced by Pfizer and Moderna, and vaccinated people with breakthrough infections can further spread the virus. Breakthrough cases caused anxiety for many as Covid transmission rose again in the United States in summer 2021. Fully vaccinated people could contract Covid-19, but this did not mean that vaccines were not working because no vaccine is 100% effective, and health authorities around the world were expecting breakthrough cases. Indeed, the real function of mRNA vaccines is to prevent severe illness and death, even from the Delta variant. Vaccines – to this end – are a form of measuring risk and reducing contagion risk as well as a form of protection against severe illness from the Delta variant, but they cannot wholly eradicate the virus itself or prevent transmission. Furthermore, it is hard to know what the post-crisis period has in store. It is not by chance that China's economy – for instance – sharply underperformed in July 2021, with widespread flooding and an outbreak of the coronavirus Delta variant strongly challenging the country's growth. And not surprisingly the answer to this phenomenon has once again been strict travel restrictions and policies in response to the largest outbreak that began in mid-July 2021 in the city of Nanjing and has since led to hundreds of new infections across multiple cities.[6] The same happened in Australia, which decided to reimpose lockdowns

6 Thomas Hale, "Delta variant and floods spark anxiety over Chinese growth" (16 August 2021) Financial Times.

threatening the country with the prospect of a double-dip recession.[7] The same negative effects of the Delta variant have been experienced in Israel, which in summer 2021 was one of the first countries in the world to experience an alarming fourth wave of infections despite 70% of its population having been jabbed by early April 2021.[8]

By the end of November 2021, a new strain of Covid-19 virus nicknamed the Omicron variant first identified in South Africa has again posed new challenges to national economies. Unfortunately, despite vaccines playing an essential role, Covid is likely to be here to stay like many other hazards or risks in our lives. It will almost certainly become endemic, continuing to spread and to flare up at different times and in different places for many years. Indeed, although the respiratory disease has had a catastrophic impact on commodity and asset prices, a recovery may not close the chapter. The coronavirus can leave a durable imprint. Indeed, variants can evade infection-induced immunity, and immunity from infection is not as strong as immunity from vaccination. Masking remains one of the ways of controlling contagion risk and infections, although with a modest effect on viral transmission.[9] However, masks are another form of managing risk and mitigating Covid infections.

This example shows that it is impossible to imagine a risk-free world, although this will always be a desired objective pursued by human beings. Risk – as we said – is everywhere and anywhere and represents the "human-humanity" of progress. Without risk and tools to measure it, society could never be able to progress and evolve in any sector, from financial markets to science. Even the strictest policy in the world cannot totally eradicate risk. Risk can be measured and curtailed, but it cannot be eradicated. Stricter policies do not equal better policies. For instance, imposing further lockdowns in a pandemic is not necessarily the best answer or the final answer to eradicating infection risk. Nonetheless, mask-wearing in public places becomes essential to try to manage infection risk. Even booster programmes after eight months from a second shot can still help to reduce risk. This shows that human beings are destined to co-habit with anxiety and risk, and especially with a subjective form of risk that is often referred to – in economic terms – as uncertainty (see Section 3.2).

3.1.1 The Epistemology of Risk

A philosophical dialogue on risk can be complex, especially from an epistemological point of view. If there is risk, something is unknown or produces an unknown result. Hence, knowledge about risk is knowledge about lack of knowledge. The

---

7 Jamie Smith, "Australia vaccine missteps keep it in the grip of Covid" (3 August 2021) Financial Times.

8 Editorial Board of Financial Times, "Israel's worrying fourth wave" (17 August 2021) Financial Times.

9 Joseph A. Ladapo, "Vaccine mandates can't stop Covid's spread" (16 September 2021) Wall Street Journal.

hendiadys of knowledge and lack of knowledge constitutes the central argument of the discourse on risk, but it explains very little about the nature of risk and the reason for its existence. Sometimes, the discourse on risk and the recognition of hendiadys can produce a tautological argument. If epistemology deals with the dissemination of knowledge in particular areas of enquiry, in relation to risk, it can be said that it is the same essence of knowledge related to a lack of knowledge that itself constitutes a limit. For this reason, the lack of knowledge that identifies the epistemology of risk points out an element of ignorance. This argument can discover a broader level of thinking in relation to the same human existence by concluding that existence itself is indeterminate and cannot be fully anticipated or controlled. This shows the finitude of human nature as well as the irremediable erroneous perception of reality. For this reason, the next question necessarily centres on the ontology of uncertainty.

3.2 The Ontology of Uncertainty

In 1731, Daniel Bernoulli introduced the concept of risk-taking. Since then, risk-taking activities have been linked to the figure of the risk-taker and the concept of risk-taking came to be seen as something that related not just to objective facts but to a subjective view concerning the desirability of the decision-making process. In other words, when something can be conceptualised as risk, the risk-taker can make a choice and decide to take that particular risk. His or her choice is determined not only by an inference decision but by opinions or judgements that are relative and subjective.

For this reason, in 1921 in the 12 chapters of 'Risk, Uncertainty and Profit', Frank Knight developed a philosophical argument concerning risk rather than a pure economic theory of profit. The subjective element of personal decisions has led thinkers to theorise a possible methodology to measure risk as something subjective and distinct from uncertainty. Furthermore, because risk cannot be prevented in any human activity, the conception of risk management has become a useful tool for identifying risk in ontological terms, and consequently influencing the subjective decisions of the risk-taker in order – this time – to be uncertainty-averse. Not only that, but risk is always a measurable uncertainty. In Knight's words:

> the practical difference between the two categories, risk and uncertainty, is that in the former the distribution of the outcome in a group of instances is known (either through calculation *a priori* or from statistics of past experience), while in the case of uncertainty this is not true (...) the best example of uncertainty is in connection with the exercise of judgement or the formation of those opinions as to the future course of the events, which opinions (and not scientific knowledge) actually guide most of our conduct.[10]

---

10 Frank Knight, *Risk, Uncertainty and Profit* (Houghton Mifflin Company 1921) 233.

Hence, knowledge about risk is knowledge of a knowable situation. We said the ontological discourse on risk represents what is knowable in principle by virtue of laws of probability and the science of statistics. By contrast, it is the judgement that is based on general principles in *a priori* probability and the opinion that is focused on perspective faculties of inference in statistical probability that gives rise to uncertainty in subjective terms. This makes the discourse on risk complex because it is not possible to measure opinions or judgements, especially if one refers to the inference or prediction processes that are only based on the projections and opinions of the agent. For these reasons, in ontological terms, uncertainty represents an immeasurable form of risk that cannot be hedged or insured against.

3.2.1 The Role of Uncertainty

Uncertainty plays a major role in financial markets as well as in life. We cannot imagine a risk-free world, simply because we cannot measure or control uncertainty. In Section 3.1.1, we said that the knowledge about risk is knowledge about lack of knowledge. This has generated a paradox according to which the knowledge of risk is a partial and imperfect knowledge. If we translated the epistemological discourse on risk to uncertainty, we would say that the knowledge of uncertainty is the knowledge of the impossible or indefinable. This shows that unlike risk, where we face an epistemological paradox, in the case of uncertainty, such knowledge becomes impossible. This means that we cannot have a subjective definition of uncertainty. We can select among different risks as a risk-taker, but we cannot select among different uncertainties. By contrast, we can only experience uncertainty. For instance, governments that are trying to manage the complex case of Covid-19 can measure the risk of new infections, but they cannot predict or measure or even select or control the uncertainty of the emergence of new variants. Nonetheless, the knowledge of uncertainty that, epistemologically, is the knowledge of the impossible can become possible once the future event has materialised in the form of risk in an infinitely recurring cycle.

3.3 The Structures of Markets

Among its other objectives, this work aims to theorise financial markets under a Luhmannian paradigm of system theory,[11] where the observation of markets defines them as financial systems. The system-environment and system-to-system constitute the point where system theory starts. A system is a system because it is different from its environment. It is capable of drawing its own borders and of

---

11 Niklas Luhmann, *Introduction to Systems Theory* (Polity Press 2013) 26. For further remarks on financial markets as financial systems see Daniele D'Alvia, *Mergers, Acquisitions, and International Financial Regulation: Analysing Special Purpose Acquisition Companies* (Routledge 2021), chapter 6.

distinguishing itself from its environment: this is what Luhmann defines as operational closure.[12] In other words, the operations that are carried out by and inside the system are capable of distinguishing it from the environment. For this reason, systems theory begins with a difference, or duality, such as in system-environment or system-non-system relations; none of the operations inside the system can be translated into the environment, and *vice versa*. Nor can any operation of the system be transplanted to other systems. It is common to speak of operational closure to express this idea of embeddedness.

Financial systems are open systems characterised by operational closure and structural coupling. Society is not inside the markets – it is external to them. Society is an important system, but it does not communicate with markets in the form of closed systems; rather, it does so exclusively in the form of open systems where effective communication between financial systems and the environment exists and is active (*i.e.* structural coupling). The structure of markets and their environment can effectively contribute to a new phenomenology of contemporary financial markets. Indeed, under this phenomenology, markets can be seen both as closed systems where the role of uncertainty is privileged and justified, and as open systems where interactions and network effects play a vital role (*i.e.* the structural coupling). Therefore, rather than perceive society as a form of closed system that is outside the market, we must begin to think of financial markets and society as forms of open systems to study the interconnections and sharing of meanings that occur between those systems. In order to understand the feature of risk and the negative outcomes that are connected to those interactions, namely those between society and the market, or better, between the environment and the system, it is useful first to argue the importance of determining the existence of a closed system inside this new phenomenology of financial markets.

Inside a closed system, there is no differentiation because closed systems are characterised by entropy-disequilibrium, though this does not mean that subject and object are not differentiated. There is a difference between subject and object but there is no form of communication between systems and environment. Therefore, the society in such a model is not affected negatively by the market's own structures, such as risk, uncertainty, competition, and financial innovation. If a financial crisis affects the market, this does not necessarily have negative welfare effects because both the society and the markets are closed systems. This is the reason why uncertainty cannot be blamed as the catalyst for a financial crisis, and by contrast, in a closed system, uncertainty becomes the leading feature of stability under disequilibrium positions. Therefore, uncertainty is the essential feature through which financial systems can achieve their spontaneous balance and equilibrium, generating, in turn, spontaneous regeneration processes in the system itself (*i.e.* autopoiesis).

The most challenging aspect of theorising financial markets as financial systems is to explain the structures of those systems. Four main structures can be identified

---

12 Luhmann (n 11) 63.

in the markets, namely risk, uncertainty, competition, and financial innovations. Therefore, it is useful to provide preliminary remarks on those structures and how they operate in financial systems, both in terms of closed and open systems. As was suggested in the previous sections, risk is an immanent feature of the world and it can be described under a "human-humanity" paradigm, whereas uncertainty is the subjective connotation of risk in terms of desirability of choices, and epistemologically the knowledge of uncertainty is the knowledge of the impossible.

To translate Luhmann's theory to financial markets, one must re-define markets as the space where risk and uncertainty exist, and where competition and financial innovation operate, in order to determine different structures. The operational closure of the system can allow the entire economy to regenerate itself. I define such financial systems as "liquid" markets or liquid financial systems because their dynamic activities tend towards the function of regeneration, and they can take as many forms as there are different structures developed inside each system. Furthermore, the operational closure of financial systems is in structural coupling with their environment. Thus, financial markets are financial systems with autopoietic mechanisms and self-organisation features that create different macro-structures, such as bond markets, equity markets, derivative markets, and so on, and micro-structures such as financial innovations, in order to appear more competitive (e.g. CoCos, SPACs, credit swaps). Furthermore, the structural coupling between the environment and financial systems is expressed in terms of meaning. The environment can influence the creation or modification of system-structures, but these cannot introduce or import their own structures. Therefore, the risk and uncertainty always present in every financial system are particular to that market and can be classified into different levels of risks and uncertainties with different features depending on the market of enquiry, such as equity or debt markets. This is the reason why debt markets are less risky than equity markets: a different level of risk is embedded. For instance, the level of risk embedded into bond markets or equity markets is due to the conditioned observation of investors who are willing to take different levels of risk depending on the markets in which they operate.

We can theorise financial systems as open systems. This is because they share meanings among themselves and their environments, but they never translate operations into other systems in order to determine new structures. Each structure of the system or market is created with its own meanings and operations. Thus, a collapse might occur in the debt market and affect borrowers' trust, but that failure cannot at the same time be translated into a corresponding collapse of the equity market, where borrowers take more risks through share investments. This is because equity and debt are two different markets and, therefore, two different financial systems. Nonetheless, structural coupling within the system-to-system relationship can produce an effect in those systems. For instance, a collapse in the mortgage subprime market, such as the notorious debt market of the 2007 financial crisis in the United States, can be translated into a selling panic effect by borrowers who own shares and seek to avoid a negative credit score. This is why financial systems are "liquid markets": they can influence each other by virtue of structural coupling.

3.3.1 The Financial Systems and Complexity

We said in Chapter 1 that in financial markets the borrower is identified as the risk-taker and the decisions of this agent are based on both objective and subjective connotations of risk. We have called the first one risk and the second uncertainty, in Knight's terms.

In general, risk can be measured through statistical assumptions, but in financial markets, risk has to be approached from an actuarial point of view. If we examine it from a purely statistical angle, a risk exists where it is statistically measurable and when probabilities can be estimated, but from an actuarial point of view, the economic consequences of these events are also important. When probability, capital, and profitability are taken into account, then financial evaluation is requested.

Classic economics introduced the idea of the risk-taker in terms of *homo economicus*, essentially the man who takes a rational decision to maximise its utility. This premise works if based on perfect information. In such a system, uncertainty is not even mentioned because every agent in the system possesses the same level of information and is capable of inferring the same data from a homogenous class of instances. Hence, variables can be predicted and anticipated. Here the science of probability explained by Knight is superfluous. To reach market equilibrium where all participants possess the same level of information, there is a need to anticipate and classify instances of risk because every class of risk is composed of homogenous instances. *Homo economicus* has become *homo stocasticus*; the man who takes decisions in terms of probability is influenced by the desirability of choices, in Bernoulli's terms. Those choices cannot be measured, and uncertainty is expressed as the unintended consequence of human action derived from ignorance and the indeterminateness of the economic system.

For this reason, the next step is to introduce the environment in which the economic agent faces risks today. This paves the way for a new phenomenology of contemporary financial markets that can be defined as a complex system dominated by risk and uncertainty and especially by competition in terms of financial innovations and adaptability. This means that in the contemporary phenomenology of financial markets, there is no central planner, and competition serves the role of de-centralised planning. In financial markets, the entrepreneur becomes the manager of the plan who by taking on responsibilities and engaging in uncertain activities contributes to money creation processes. In other words, it can be said that the entrepreneur explains the function of absorbing uncertainty from the system. This means that if the subjectivity of financial risk is intelligible but not knowable due to its necessarily unknowable nature (*i.e.* uncertainty), the future, at least in contemporary financial markets, is no longer perceived as an opportunity, but as something that is feared and must be controlled. Since the collapse of Lehman Brothers in 2008 and the start of the 2007–2010 Global Financial Crisis, and even more today with Covid-19, uncertainty-aversion has dominated the markets, but the management and correct pricing of risk in its objective dimension is still vital for governing markets.[13] As a result, the risk-taker who sees the future as an opportunity has shifted to an uncertainty-aversion paradigm by means of what can be defined as the contemporary phenomenology of financial markets, where their subjectivity has suspended and overwhelmed the objective realism of their own ontology. The figure of the speculator has contributed to the current financial crisis, while, on the other hand, supervisors and financial regulators cannot be blamed for their actions insofar as they are inside the disaster myopia discourse.[14]

3.3.2 Competition and Financial Innovation

In economic terms, complexity is associated with uncertainty. Something complex cannot be controlled, and therefore cannot be predicted. Our need to reduce complexity is expressed in modern economies in the anxiety to reduce economic uncertainty. This is because by reducing uncertainty things seem more predictable, and from an epistemological point of view, the knowledge of uncertainty is based on the conception of a "controllable" feature, although – as we said – this is impossible. Nonetheless, a free-risk world cannot be feasible, nor can a financial system that has perfect information be projected or imagined due to the innate information asymmetry of markets. Future events have revealed a subjective element of financial risk that is relative rather than absolute: uncertainty.

For these reasons, it is important to take into account uncertainty from an ontological point of view. Reducing complexity does not only mean reducing profit; as per Knight, uncertainty tends to underpin rather than undermine money creation processes. To reduce uncertainty means to reduce competition – that is the one feature or structure that makes each financial system adaptable. Indeed, competition has two sides: on the one hand, it represents the dark side of modern economies in relation to financial crisis or business collapse (for example, if businesses are not adaptable and innovative enough, they are out of the market, or alternatively too much innovation can generate new financial risks that might be unsustainable), and, on the other hand, it creates innovation that makes the system adapt to a new environment. Therefore, complexity is a process, and competition leads to a free market's complexity in terms of identifying the right risk opportunity, profiting from it, and innovating the system.

3.4 The New Legal Theory of Finance

The main question is still whether the market and its operators can govern uncertainty and provide the economic system with reliable answers. However, as anticipated in the earlier sections, uncertainty is one of the four structures of the

---

13 Claudio Borio, Haibin Zhu, "Capital regulation, risk-taking and monetary policy: A missing link in the transmission mechanism?" (2008) 268 BIS Working Papers 3.
14 Jack Guttentag, Richard Herring, "Disaster myopia in international banking" (1986) 164 *Essays in International Finance*, Princeton University Press.

financial system, and it directly relates to money-making processes. For this reason, the role of uncertainty must not be underestimated because it is a central idea for profit realisation, and it is important – as we have seen – for the activation of a spontaneous mechanism of market regeneration (autopoiesis). However, financial markets are also complex entities. This means that financial systems are open systems that communicate with their environment, although they are characterised by an operation closure by which structures of the environment cannot be imported inside the system.

This idea is challenging, and it gives rise to a new role for law-making where the system itself develops and enacts its own regulation. The idea of fragmented knowledge is Ladeur's central point of assertion to recognise the end of a centralised stock of knowledge administrated by the state. As opposed to a Westphalian model of legislation, modern society is characterised by the "a-centric" creation of order, and no central planner is contemplated within this new globalised framework.[15] For Ladeur, this means recognising society as a "network of networks" (a term he borrowed from Eli M. Noam).[16] In other words, society is no longer based on hierarchical forms of power, but on heterarchical relationships aimed at creating, rather than individualism, a spontaneous process of cooperation. For this reason, one side effect of this cooperation is the establishment of a collective order that is the product of self-organisation behaviours in society; so the law becomes merely a secondary instrument of integration that is no longer characterised by its authoritative conception as a form of mediation of consensus. Furthermore, the law has a political connotation that is embedded into super-structures such as states' constitutions. In this example, the constitution represents a political instrument or declaration of rights that creates a super-structure within the legal order because the constitution represents the supreme law of the state, the source of legitimisation of every other legal provision, in terms of Kelsen's *Grundnorm*.[17]

3.4.1 The Un(codified) Role of Uncertainty

If the knowledge of uncertainty is the knowledge of the impossible, it is logical to assert that uncertainty cannot be codified. In other words, you cannot codify something that you do not know. However, we have seen uncertainty is probably the most important structure of financial systems in their operational closure because it can sustain market regeneration processes. Furthermore, uncertainty from a structural coupling point of view is the structure that allows the rediscovery of the creative role of competition and financial innovation.

15 Karl-Heinz Ladeur, "The financial market crisis – a case of network failure?" in Kjaer, Teubner, Febbrajo (eds) *The Financial Crisis in Constitutional Perspective: The Dark Side of Functional Differentiation* (Hart Publishing 2011) 78.
16 Eli M. Noam, *Interconnecting the Network of Networks* (MIT Press 2001).
17 Hans Kelsen, *General Theory of Law and State* (The Lawbook exchange 1945).

On the other hand, uncertainty is also the trigger that has changed the role of the law. Law today is the "output" rather than the "input" in the absence of a central planner. This new connotation of the law in a marginalised role is the direct product of uncertainty. The lawmaker cannot predict the future or control uncertain events; especially if financial innovations are growing fast as a symptom of market regeneration, the law cannot keep pace. For this reason, uncertainty is not only determining a new formation of structures within financial systems by virtue of autopoiesis, but also a new codification process through which uncodified common meanings by virtue of interpretation are found inside non-legal words, legal provisions, or decisions that are the results of new heterarchical relationships. Once agreed at international level, those forms of cooperation and common meanings are embedded in hard law provisions of national legal frameworks (for instance, the reform of national insolvency frameworks based on the insolvency law assessments of international organisations or multilateral institutions at international level); hard law provisions at the same international level (e.g. the Restructuring Directive); and quasi-legal frameworks and soft law instruments (the UNCITRAL Model Law on Cross-Border Insolvency, and the other documents, principles, and recommendations outlined in Chapter 4). This is the new role of legal constants as explained in Chapter 2 and throughout this work. (Legal) constants rather than the law are the unique instances of the new uncodified-codification process of the law.

3.5 Conclusions

In this chapter, a possible re-definition of free markets has been described for the first time in the new paradigm of the phenomenology of contemporary financial markets. We have identified markets as systems under Luhmann's system theory, so financial markets are financial systems and, specifically, they are open systems.

Within a first and second level of observation in Luhmann's conception, I have re-interpreted the manifestation of financial systems in their original forms as closed systems. Here, it is possible to identify "what financial markets are", and I have argued that markets are determined by three main features: uncertainty, competition, and financial innovation. However, this is only a model theory and cannot actually reflect the complexity of the reality. For this, we need a metaphysical description of markets under the heading "what is experienced in financial systems". This reveals a new stage of thinking where financial systems are open systems and financial risk dominates the scene. Financial risk has been privatised and under-priced, giving rise to credit bubbles, but it is that same experience of financial risk that creates profit; so, the risk-taker or entrepreneur is a profit-maker, and his willingness to make a profit turns the uncertainty that permeates the markets into risk opportunity so that profit becomes a way of absorbing uncertainty.

I define the financial systems that are open systems as "liquid markets" because they can influence each other by means of structural coupling. Nonetheless, each financial system's operation is strictly confined within the same system, and it cannot be transferred into the environment or another system. Operational closure is the right term, in the view of Luhmann, to identify this feature of modernity. Indeed, in modern economies, liquid autopoietic markets are determined by a web of connections and mechanisms of cooperation because of their open systems, but, at the same time, the environment cannot influence the markets' operations. In other words, markets can regenerate themselves as a response to external stimuli through operational closure and effectively implement a process of autopoiesis where financial structures are reformed and spontaneously re-created to achieve new economic equilibria.

4 Cross-Border Insolvency Law
Venturing Beyond Structural Crisis

4.1 International Insolvency Law

This chapter describes instances of soft law that are especially relevant in a Covid-19 scenario and that are expected to shape the legal and financial world in years to come.

Because this book is focused on international insolvency and finance law, we will focus on the legal frameworks and international benchmarks of the EBRD Core Principles of Insolvency (Core Principles), the World Bank Principles for Effective Insolvency and Creditor/Debtor Regimes (Principles), and the UNCITRAL Legislative Guide to Insolvency Law to discover how they represent legal constants in times of crisis. Also, the World Bank and the UNCITRAL, in consultation with the International Monetary Fund, designed the Insolvency Creditor Rights Standard (ICR Standard) to represent the international consensus on best practices for evaluating and strengthening national insolvency and creditor rights systems. The ICR Standard does this by combining the World Bank and the UNCITRAL Legislative Guide on Insolvency Law. The Financial Stability Board has recognised and designated the ICR Standard as one of the key standards for sound financial systems and deserving of priority implementation depending on countries' circumstances.

However, what will be said in this chapter can also be said in respect of other areas of the law such as environmental law, energy law, corporate governance law, and so on. This is because those areas of the law are likewise highly influenced and modified by international practices and soft law instruments that are always more focused on promoting and conceiving non-legal meanings.

This chapter introduces the legal models, or better, quasi-legal instruments through which domestic legislations are subject to modifications. Those models also represent venues through which constant(s) outside of the law get access to the legal sphere. They are examples of soft law and are non-binding. However, those principles can be "codified" inside domestic binding legislations. These are the roles of global legal indicators and legal assessments: namely to influence hard law-making processes through the identification of common commercial out-of-law concepts that must find a "legal space" for implementation. These are further instances of the "uncodified-codification" of the law, and this is how evidence is

DOI: 10.4324/9781003278320-5

collected to support the claim that the law is the "output" of any "uncodified-cod-ification" process beyond structural financial crisis. To this end, a measurement of progress in legal reforms is to assess both the current laws "on the books" (*i.e.* extensiveness) and how these laws work in practice (*i.e.* effectiveness). Reviewing the black letter of the law and analysing how these laws are applied reveals non-legal meanings that in turn generate further (legal) constant(s).

4.1.1 The Role of Contract Law versus Statute Law

When a business is in financial difficulties, it should be addressed at an early stage. As we anticipated in Chapter 1, this is critical for a successful turnaround; early restructuring can maximise the total value to creditors, employees, owners, and the economy as a whole. In Chapter 2, we highlighted that this new approach, determined by a rescue culture, is indirectly informed by a contractarian view of insolvency law focusing on finding the right balance with creditors' bargaining power. The emerging role of contract law in insolvency practices has a long history and can even be viewed as exceptional to established rules and law principles in insolvency law, especially regarding the principle of *pari passu.*

In corporate insolvency law, the common denominators to protect creditors' interests are the duty to provide the same treatment to creditors (*par condicio creditorum*), respect pre-insolvency entitlements, and observe the principle of *pari passu,* according to which each creditor is paid equally and without prefer-ence in the distribution of any available debtor assets, or proceeds of sale from those assets, in proportion to the debts due to each creditor. The objectives of the *pari passu* principle are commonly considered to be fairness and the orderly distribution of assets.[1] This reflects the public policy that an insolvency regime should not be displaced by private arrangements (at least in theory). In other words, the application of the *pari passu* principle means that under insolvency law, an insolvent company's estate must be distributed equally among creditors on a *pro rata* basis. Such a principle is mandatory in many jurisdictions, for exam-ple, in English law by section 107 Insolvency Act 1986 for voluntary liquidation, and under rule 14.12 Insolvency (England and Wales) Rules 2016 for compulsory liquidation. While commentators such as Goode[2] have described the principle as "fundamental" in theory, in reality, it is subject to a large number of exceptions.

At the national level, there is an intricate web of exceptions to the principle of *pari passu,* which vary across jurisdictions and aim at protecting specific classes of creditors. In other words, to protect superior interests, the lawmaker in almost every legal system creates exceptions to the general principle of equality. For

---

1   *Report of the Review Committee on Insolvency Law and Practice* (1982) Cmnd 8558, also known as the Cork Report was an investigation and set of recommendations on modernisation and reform of UK Insolvency Law chaired by Kenneth Cork and commissioned by the Labour Government in 1977. The Cork Report was followed by a White Paper in 1984: *A Revised Framework for Insol-vency Law* (1984) Cmnd 9175 and these led to the Insolvency Act 1986.

2   Roy Goode, *Principles of Corporate Insolvency Law* (Sweet & Maxwell 1997).

instance, statutory orders of priorities exist in insolvency proceedings that allow certain creditors to be paid before others in the event of a corporate liquidation (namely, insolvency expenses, salaries, or taxes must be paid before any other debt). The law aims at ensuring that the legal procedure can be completed, and that liquidation does not cause excessive social harm to employees or diminish tax revenues on the side of the state. In those exceptions, it is possible to see the classic role of the law as "input" where specific interests are codified by virtue of legal means. This is a direct example of the "Code of Capital" that Pistor is arguing for; the final question being, in her view, who decides and who has the discretionary power to discriminate among creditors' interest? In short, the state, which sits at the apex of the system where, she argues, exists the necessary flexibility to adopt decisions that sometimes might even go against the protection of other interests such as those of unsecured creditors in an insolvency proceeding. The codification of capital is clear in those examples.

However, orders of priorities are not exclusively created by the law, and therefore, by the state. We could say that the "codification" of interests in insolvency law procedures is not necessarily based on the law. Indeed, the principle of *pari passu* can also be – and in practice often is – altered through contract law and the private autonomy of parties. A lender can ask for a security over a borrower's asset to grant a loan. Indeed, after a credit assessment of the borrower measuring its solvability risk, a creditor can ask for collateral in order to ensure that he will get paid. By using a security, the creditor moves up the waterfall of repayments since he will be paid in priority, provided that the debtor has enough assets to cover the losses until the corresponding rank is reached. Conversely, a creditor may want to be moved into a worse position through subordination in order to benefit from higher interest rates. Hence, the *pari passu* principle seems to be disregarded not only by the law itself but also in contractual arrangements. A creditor may want to have a lower ranking in the waterfall of payments because although this desire is counter-intuitive, it can be justified by financial interests. The lower rank equates to higher interest rates because the probability of not getting paid is higher. The higher the risk, the higher the return is the main feature of debt and leverage finance. In the creditors' ranking, after senior creditors come second liens, followed by mezzanine and high yield debt. Creditors holding this last kind of loan are usually referred to as junior creditors. Hedge funds – for instance – are attracted by these loans because they tend to invest in high-risk assets.

In essence, using collaterals is the reverse of the *pari passu* principle. This is why it is sometimes said that the *pari passu* principle exists among unsecured or ordinary creditors. Secured creditors change the equal ranking among creditors. During a liquidation, a debtor's assets are sold through auction and the overall amount is collected by the liquidator, who then distributes them among the creditors. Secured creditors have a collateral over a certain type of assets. For example, the collateral can be a mortgage for real estate or a pledge over shares. Creditors holding a security, also named senior creditors, are entitled to collect the amount obtained by selling the collateralised assets. Thus, they "jump" the queue in comparison to other ordinary creditors, namely those who do not hold any collateral.

On the other hand, being placed higher in the hierarchy of repayments has a cost: secured creditors have lower interest rates than creditors that do not hold any collateral. Sometimes lenders that do not find an agreement on taking out a security ask for a covenant in the facility agreement called a negative pledge clause. Through this clause, the debtor undertakes to not provide any pledge on his assets to other lenders. This type of clause restores the equality of rank among creditors, which shows that contract law does not always alter it.

Finally, another contractual form to reorganise the principle of *pari passu* focuses on the function of inter-creditor agreements (ICAs). In modern transactions, particularly those related to leveraged buy-out, numerous creditors will grant loans to one single debtor (the special purpose vehicle or SPV). The acquisition of a large company can be quantified in a deal worth millions or sometimes billions; a single creditor alone cannot provide such a facility to the debtor, so a group of creditors comes together to finance the acquisition. Creditors will likely agree to enter into an ICA to settle their relations. This contract contains one main provision to modify the *pari passu* clause: the waterfall provision. This stipulates that creditors are ranked from senior to high yield. It also simplifies the relations between borrowers and lenders as they nominate a creditors' agent and a security agent who are generally senior creditors. Those agents mutualise the interests of all creditors by being the direct interlocutor with the borrower. The main rationale of the ICA is to avoid the court's involvement in case of failure of repayment by the debtor. The relation between parties is already dictated by the ICA and, in theory, there is no need for the parties to go to court to settle the dispute since the repayment order has already been established by the ICA. However, in practice, the negotiation process of an ICA is often distorted. Senior creditors tend to have a stronger position than juniors, so in practice ICAs are more favourable to senior creditors, and they tend to increase the enforceability of the senior creditors' collaterals. Indeed, once the borrower becomes insolvent, senior creditors are likely to force the sale of the collateralised assets while ensuring that junior creditors have no claims over these assets in order to obtain the highest possible price at auction. To do so, provisions called release clauses are inserted into ICAs which authorise the security agent to get rid of all claims that junior lenders may have over secured assets during an auction process. Hence, according to Hooley, an additional layer of alteration is brought by contract law to the *pari passu* principle, as junior parties to ICA simply have no claim over secured assets and often find themselves "out of the money".[3]

There is evidence in the American and English case law that ICAs can be enforced, further demonstrating how, at least in these common law jurisdictions, private contracting can alter equal ranking. For instance, in a landmark English decision (*Re Maxwell Communications Corporation Plc* [1993]), it was argued that the *pari passu* distribution of assets among unsecured creditors was a general

---

3 Richard Hooley, "Release provisions in inter-creditor agreements" (2012) 3 Journal of Business Law 213.

rule of insolvency law from which it was not possible to contract out, even to one's own disadvantage, particularly by analogy with cases on set-off in insolvency. The court held that this was not the law. There was no reason why a particular creditor should not waive his right to prove altogether or save to the extent of assets remaining after another creditor is satisfied, and that they could do this either in the insolvency or in advance of it. In other words, a secured creditor can lower their ranking if they have so agreed. Mokal argues that this decision makes it evident that the principle of *pari passu* is "far from sacrosanct".[4]

On the other hand, *Ion Media* was the first case in a series of bankruptcy court decisions since the GFC to rule on the enforceability of prepetition ICAs among lenders, and to a certain extent, it set the stage for decisions going forward. The ICA was enforceable where second lien and junior lenders challenged the validity of the first lien lenders' purported lien over debtor property, contested the priority scheme established, and objected to a reorganisation plan consistent with that scheme. It was held that by entering the ICA, the second lien lenders had contractually waived their standing to challenge the validity of the particular licences, demonstrating that waivers of rights in the ICA would be enforced, putting first lien lenders in a strong position.

Those cases show how while common law countries have an approach to contracting as *caveat emptor*, meaning the junior creditors should be aware of the agreement they entered into, civil law jurisdictions may favour protection of their interests to preserve fairness and apply the principle of good faith. However, even intuitively, it seems unfair to bring balance into the picture when parties have freely consented to enter the contract. Private autonomy matters, especially under French or Italian law. As long as there has not been fraud and misrepresentation on the part of contracting parties, their agreement should be honoured and fulfilled.

Finally, this in turn provides direct evidence of how the meanings derived from the principle of good faith that we explored in Chapter 2 can lead to different interpretations and the instauration of different (legal) constants between common law and civil law countries in interpreting exceptions to the *pari passu* principle.

4.2 The Global Legal Indicators

As they are unceasingly *à la recherche* of innovative approaches to the study of the law, comparative legal studies engage in intense cross-disciplinary research. This is also the case with what Mathias Siems terms as "numerical comparative law",[5] which provides comparative scholars with the idea of measuring and assessing the law against allegedly scientific benchmarks. Legal indicators (or

---

4 Riz Mokal, "Priority as pathology: The pari passu myth" (2001) 60 (3) Cambridge Law Journal 581.
5 Mathias Siems, *Comparative Law* (2nd edn, CUP 2018).

leximetrics) assess how change affects several ambits of the legal spectrum.[6] Through them, legal scholars and policy-makers measure legal systems against specific benchmarks; they no longer search for commonalities among legal systems but are interested in assessing how the law performs in economic terms. And the ranking of legal systems depends on how they ensure such elevated economic performance. Doing numerical comparative law and adopting quantitative methods allow policy-makers and technocrats to rank the "quality" of legal systems so that they may match the unceasing need to achieve higher returns. The metrics acts as an alternative source of legitimisation and law-making, triggering transformative changes in several jurisdictions, which indeed adopt legal reforms in diverse areas of their legal system to match the level of performativity which is "suggested" by both benchmarks and indexes. The way indicators are framed, used, and promoted in transnational contexts becomes the fabric of economic comfort zones, *i.e.* legal spaces where financial risk inherent to investment and business venture is reduced or made predictable (the laws of probability in terms of risk-measuring in Chapter 3).

In other words, to predict the future means to use managerial rationality. This has had a pervasive influence on the law in our society. Generally speaking, indicators have been associated with a culture of performance and auditing.[7] A performance measure is broadly defined as a

> general term applied to a part of the conduct of the activities of an organisation over a period of time, often with reference to some standard or base with emphasis on management responsibility and accountability, or the like.[8]

We have to acknowledge that the idea of performance measures is not new. In *Principles of Scientific Management*, Frederick Taylor describes the different levels that quantification, systematisation, and what we would today call benchmarking lead to the definition of single standards that can be replicated in industrial processes or in engineering.

In terms of legal indicators, the same approach is endorsed, for instance, by the Rule of Law Index, which claims to measure the extent to which countries attain the rule of law in practice by means of performance indicators[9] or the CSR Corporate Social Responsibility performance for a broad range of companies. Essentially, global legal indicators are a subcategory of social indicators, which

---

6 Ralf Michaels, "Comparative law by numbers? Legal origins thesis, doing business reports, and the silence of traditional comparative law" (2009) 57 (4) The American Journal of Comparative Law 765–769.

7 Kevin Davis, Benedict Kingsbury, Sally Engle Merry, "The local-global life of indicators: Law, power, and resistance" in Merry, Davis, Kingsbury (eds) *The Quiet Power of Indicators: Measuring Governance Corruption and the Rule of Law* (Cambridge University Press 2015).

8 James Edwards, *The Use of Performance Measures* (Montvale: National Association of Accountants 1986) 5.

9 World Justice Project, *Rule of Law Index* (2016).

includes measures, standards, and ranking of the quality of law and legal institutions across the world, in particular regions or in selected jurisdictions.[10] It has been argued that global legal indicators are an integral part of a system of management control based on a broader set of institutional practices and networks:

> Performance management and measurement relies on a simple and fundamental assumption: "You get what you measure". However, simply measuring performance is not enough as measures can be manipulated and almost always mask dysfunctional behaviour effects. Measurement must therefore be integrated into a management system, for which it can serve as an objective and clear starting point, but which it cannot replace.[11]

When managerial practices reach international law, the politics behind it are hidden. This is the managerial rationality that informs the legal sphere and is not in competition with politics, but a substitute for it.[12] However, legal indicators are not traditional managerial measures, and their legitimacy is based on a cycle of production and implementation. The cycle is divided into four processes: data-producing, benchmarking, auditing, and attributing incentives.[13] Each of them participates in the legitimacy of legal indicators.[14] The following sections, therefore, analyse the final process by which legal indicators are implemented in insolvency law guides that, in turn, serve the purpose of influencing and modifying the legal space of national economies.

4.2.1 The UNCITRAL Legislative Guide on Insolvency Law

UNCITRAL is a subsidiary body of the General Assembly of the United Nations, which was established in 1966 with the general mandate to further the progressive harmonisation and unification of international trade law. UNCITRAL has prepared a Legislative Guide on Insolvency Law that seeks to present a broad and general description of the objectives and key features that all insolvency regimes should have, and the criteria to be followed both in legal relations between debtors and creditors and in cases of out-of-court reorganisations of companies.

In order to meet its objectives, the Legislative Guide on Insolvency Law presents several recommendations concerning the criteria and solutions to be followed by countries in order to contribute to the creation of an effective and efficient legal framework to regulate the situation of debtors in financial difficulties.

---

10 Frederick Taylor, *Globalisation and Legal Theory* (Cambridge University Press 2000) 254.
11 Helene Loning, Veronique Malleret, Jerome Meric, and Yvon Pesquex, *Performance Management and Control* (Dunod 2016) 157–158.
12 Matti Koskenniemi, "The fate of public international law: Between technique and politics" (2007) 70 Modern Law Review 1–30.
13 Loning et al. (n 11).
14 David Restrepo Amariles, "Supping with the Devil? Indicators and the rise of managerial rationality in law" (2017) 13 (4) International Journal of Law in Context 465–484.

In turn, it reflects modern developments and trends in the area of insolvency law. Additionally, the Legislative Guide on Insolvency Law stresses that, in order to achieve proper development of an insolvency regime, it is not only necessary to provide the latter with an adequate legal framework but also with appropriate infrastructure and resources to allow the process to develop efficiently. In light of this, the Legislative Guide on Insolvency Law seeks to serve as a guide for countries by proposing recommendations for the different problems that occur in most insolvency regimes and establishing common guidelines for solving them.

It is important to highlight that among the main recommendations given by the Legislative Guide on Insolvency Law, the special emphasis that it places on the treatment of secured creditors within insolvency proceedings, and therefore the importance that any legal framework should give to these types of creditors in order to protect them. UNCITRAL also recommends that any insolvency law should include provisions governing both the reorganisation and the liquidation of a debtor, as well as establishing that where a security right is effective and enforceable under a rule outside the insolvency law, it must also be recognised in insolvency proceedings.

Similarly, any insolvency law should provide for a modern, harmonised, and fair framework for the effective settlement of cross-border insolvency cases. To this end, it is recommended that countries incorporate in their domestic law the UNCITRAL Model Law on Cross-Border Insolvency, in order to recognise claims and rights arising under national or foreign norms outside the insolvency law, subject to the limitations expressly foreseen in each case.

For example, the importance of the Model Law on Cross-Border Insolvency can be appreciated in a recent decision in late 2021 by a Brazilian court to recognise proceedings in Singapore for the restructuring of Prosafe SE and its Singaporean subsidiary Prosafe Rigs Pte Ltd. The decision is the first instance of recognition of a foreign insolvency proceeding by a Brazilian court since Brazil adopted the UNCITRAL Model Law on Cross-Border Insolvency. As economies and companies around the globe continue to face financial difficulties due to the Covid-19 pandemic, one might expect further instances of recognition of foreign insolvency proceedings in Brazil and elsewhere, although several countries in Europe have not yet adopted this framework, with the exception of a few such as Romania, Greece, Poland, the UK, and Slovenia. Specifically, in Europe, the UNCITRAL Model Law on Cross-Border Insolvency may be adopted in addition to the European Regulation on Insolvency Proceedings, which applies directly to cross-border insolvency procedures where the debtor has a centre of main interests in the European Union. This may be supplemented by the adoption of the UNCITRAL Model Law on Recognition and Enforcement of Insolvency-Related Judgements, which further assists the conduct of cross-border insolvency proceedings and increases the potential for successful reorganisation or liquidation.

These models are a guide, and states enacting legislation based upon a model law have the flexibility to depart from the text. Hence, each state's legislation should be considered in order to identify the exact nature of any possible deviation from the model in the adopted legislative text. This confirms our intuition on (legal) constants, according to which common or shared meanings might still be influenced by national law principles or rules (see Chapter 2). Once the common meaning has been identified as a sort of benchmark, then national provisions can still influence the interpretation of a legal transplant.

According to the recommendations of the Legislative Guide on Insolvency Law, any insolvency legal system should have the following fundamental objectives:

1. Provision of certainty in the market to promote economic stability and growth.
2. Maximisation of the value of assets.
3. Striking a balance between liquidation and reorganisation.
4. Ensuring equitable treatment of similarly situated creditors.
5. Provision for timely, efficient, and impartial resolution of insolvency.
6. Preservation of the insolvency estate to allow equitable distribution to creditors.
7. Ensuring a transparent and predictable insolvency law that contains incentives for gathering and dispensing information.
8. Recognition of existing creditor rights and the establishment of clear rules for the ranking of priority claims.
9. Establishment of a framework for cross-border insolvency.

UNCITRAL proposes some basic features that any insolvency law must incorporate in order to be able to develop an effective and efficient framework. In particular, UNCITRAL is in the process of finalising the adoption of a Model Law on Micro-Small-Medium-Enterprise Insolvency.

4.2.2 The World Bank Principles for Effective Insolvency and Creditor/Debtor Regimes

The Principles for Effective Insolvency and Creditor Rights prepared by the World Bank Group are a synthesis of international best practices in the design of insolvency systems and creditor rights. They have been designed as a broad-spectrum evaluation tool in order to assist countries in their efforts to assess and improve key aspects of their systems of commercial law, fundamental for a healthy investment climate, and to promote economic and commercial growth. Effective, credible, and transparent creditors' rights and insolvency systems are vitally important for achieving the redistribution of productive resources in the entrepreneurial sector for investor confidence and long-term corporate reorganisation.

Insolvency systems also play a key role in times of crisis in that they enable a country and its stakeholders to respond quickly and resolve business financial issues on a systemic scale.

The Principles were created in 2001 in response to the emerging markets crisis in the late 1990s. From its inception until its first revision in 2005, the World Bank has been in contact with a variety of international organisations, countries, and cross-border operators to assess the practical experience and application of the Principles, aiming at introducing improvements to improve their effectiveness. Further revisions took place in 2011, 2015, and 2021. The 2005 revision grouped the principles under relevant headings to provide a streamlined approach. The 2011 revision incorporated the updates made to the UNCITRAL Legislative Guide on Insolvency Law to reflect best international practices in the regulation of the insolvency of enterprise groups. In 2015, changes were made to the Principles, highlighting the relationship between the cost and flow of credit (including secured credit) and the laws and institutions that recognise and enforce credit agreements. Also, and in line with the UNCITRAL Legislative Guide on Insolvency, the Principles enlarged the scope of the duties and responsibilities of the directors in a distress scenario.

Finally, in 2021, the WBG prepared the last revision of the Principles with a specific focus on helping policymakers build and improve the insolvency and bankruptcy systems that support the micro, small, and medium enterprises that have been particularly hard-hit by the Covid-19 crisis. Micro and SMEs represent over 60% of private sector employment globally and need efficient, cost-effective insolvency principles in order to either successfully restructure or exit the market.

4.2.3 The EBRD Core Principles of an Effective Insolvency System

The EBRD's Legal Transition Programme (LTP) has conducted a number of assessments of the state of transition in the EBRD region in selected areas of commercial law, including insolvency, seeking to assess the law and legal systems of the EBRD countries of operations. Assessments of commercial legal frameworks play an important role in monitoring the status of legal transition and legal risk for investments, identifying priorities for the Bank's policy engagement, and contributing to further commercial law reforms and development. To this end, the role of a well-designed insolvency framework in facilitating the extension of credit and private sector development is widely recognised.[15]

The LTP led assessment of insolvency laws in 2003–2004 and repeated the assessment in 2006, 2009, and 2020. Since the 2009 assessment, there has been a significant level of insolvency law reform globally. This shows the practical importance of such insolvency law assessments as well as the new emerging role of comparative law as a policy instrument to modify national legislations. As we examined in Chapter 1 and at the start of this chapter, recent insolvency reforms have been driven in great measure by the GFC and subsequent economic downturn and a renewed emphasis on the role and importance of insolvency systems in maintaining financial stability.

The general objective of most insolvency systems is the efficient liquidation of non-viable businesses and the rescue of viable businesses in temporary financial difficulties. Specifically, since the EBRD's 2009 insolvency assessment,

---

15 See, for example, the foreword to the 2021 World Bank "Principles for effective insolvency and creditor/debtor regimes" published in 2021.

insolvency law reform has focused increasingly on encouraging early restructuring by the debtor and avoiding a full-blown insolvency procedure. However, in many countries, restructuring procedures are not used in practice (e.g. Bulgaria) or are used by some debtors as a means of delaying an inevitable liquidation (e.g. Hungary). This confirms the relevance and feasibility of running an assessment of the expediency and facilitation of reorganisation options in the region of the EBRD, which is keen to promote further development of insolvency legislation to encourage reorganisation in its countries of operations. Specifically, in recent years, there has been an increasing focus on the importance of statutory restructuring tools, consensual out-of-court restructuring solutions, and early "pre-insolvency" action to support business continuity.

For these reasons, and because the needs and dynamics change over time, the periodicity of insolvency law assessments (ILAs) is fundamental. Croatia, Egypt, Georgia, Kazakhstan, Latvia, Lithuania, Moldova, Poland, Romania, Serbia, Slovenia, Tunisia, and Ukraine are among EBRD countries of operations that have substantially reformed their insolvency laws in recent years.

In 2020, the EBRD started a new ILA. This is also a well-timed assessment for EBRD countries of operations which either are EU member states or are EU accession countries. Indeed, the Restructuring Directive requires member states to ensure that debtors in financial difficulty have access to an effective preventive restructuring framework that enables them to restructure their debts or business, restore their viability, and avoid insolvency. The directive, therefore, calls for member states to review their insolvency framework for reorganisation.

To this end, the ILA is a comparative tool to highlight major weaknesses that should be addressed by national legislators in order to improve the efficiency of the insolvency framework with respect to the expedience and facilitation of its reorganisation, and gauge the effectiveness of a country's insolvency law, benchmarked against international best practice: for instance, the Restructuring Directive and the Principles of the WBG serve as a benchmark to measure the legislative performance of national insolvency law frameworks. Finally, to reflect those developments in terms of best practice, in 2020, the EBRD also updated its Core Principles of an Effective Insolvency System, first published 15 years ago. The Core Principles do not deal with financial institutions but focus just on corporate rescue and cross-border insolvency in relation to companies and SMEs. Particularly important, *inter alia*, is Principle n. 15 on cross-border insolvency, which encourages countries to adopt the UNCITRAL Model Law on Cross-Border Insolvency, confirming how insolvency procedures can become effective if a mutual recognition of judgements is in place.

4.3 The New Financial Architecture

We have seen how the law has played a limited role in preventing financial crises since the inception of the GFC. More regulation does not necessarily imply more transparent or more efficient markets. I argue that a Westphalian approach to regulation based exclusively on state law can be superseded by a self-regulatory approach where soft law becomes "harder". This can generate spontaneous mechanisms of compliance, and a voluntary model of self-regulation inspired by market practices and knowledge of financial operators; this has already occurred in other areas of the law (for instance, the Takeover Code in the UK, the international financial regulation of Special Purpose Acquisition Companies, mobile payments, and de-centralised finance with smart contracts). Pistor, in the "Code of Capital", claims that financial operators, instead of using self-regulatory approaches, are working towards the codification of the future by enacting a digital code. Even this affirmation is misleading because no legal provision, today, is capable of keeping up the fast pace of technological improvements. The knowledge of uncertainty is the knowledge of the impossible, as we claimed in Chapter 3 when we examined the epistemological meaning of uncertainty in financial markets. Hence, the law cannot be conceived as the "input" of a codification process that tends to qualify facts in legal terms. By contrast, we must start from the facts, from the non-legal meanings and the out-of-law space in order to identify constants with a common meaning for different markets and financial operators. In light of this, the law can keep track of the future by initiating uncodified facts into a codification process that does not follow the traditional path of state regulation. For these reasons, the "uncodified-codification" of the law is in direct opposition to Pistor's views on codification and comparative law: following those lines, a universal digital code might or might not exist depending on the constant meanings that international financial operators and organisations will tend to follow or recognise in their quasi-legal frameworks or hard law frameworks.

The failure of direct codification through macro-legislations that tend to echo Pistor's "universal" code can further sustain the argument that uncertainty governs the markets (see Chapter 3). For these reasons, uncertainty-aversion paradigms are obsolete and where uncertainty has been rejected, consequently profits have dropped too. Hence, the uncodified uncertainty in the Covid-19 crisis is a primary example of how no codification process can ignore the importance of out-of-law instances in the act of making law. Additionally, this trend has given rise to democratic, discriminatory, and participatory concerns as well as to the establishment of an ambiguous legal status for private organisations or non-state actors such as the IMF, WBG, and UNCITRAL. Apart from these political issues that hybrid regulation gives rise to and result from the process of privatisation of financial risk, the hybrid feature of the system makes the involvement of private actors a fundamental instance of regulatory responses as opposed to governments or governmental agencies that are part of the public sphere. In the absence of a supreme architect of the financial system or a central planner, the necessary de-centralisation of the financial environment allows for new heterarchical relationships to be formed (see Chapters 1 and 3).

4.3.1 Macro- versus Micro-Legislations

It is fair to say that the endemic failure of markets implies that there is a need for regulation or supervision. However, as this chapter has evidenced, the paternalistic role of the state has been irreversibly modified towards a new global governance paradigm in financial markets. If internal capital controls are reduced or eliminated, then domestic firms gain more room for taking financial risk. This theoretically is not an issue as long as there is perfect competition and perfect information in the market. However, markets always register a lack of perfect information. Furthermore, the lack of theoretical grounds for the justification that self-regulated markets can achieve market equilibrium alone has always enabled the idea of top-down government intervention. To this end, the theory of Adam Smith that markets can be efficiently self-governed by an "invisible hand" has always been contrasted with the Westphalian system, a model based on a paternalistic view of the state in which regulation is imposed from the top as an expression of classic state sovereignty. This view is also capable of influencing the expansion of domestic markets through legal impositions and internal capital controls.

One of the most relevant features of financial markets today is that they are not exclusively based on state regulation, but rather on private actors' decisions and inter-agency forums that give rise to hybrid forms of regulation. In other words, today, the current dynamics of markets refer to a conception of global governance where it is not possible to rely exclusively on states' intervention to govern complex financial markets. The final outcome of the regulation process is the result of at least a mixture of sources, deriving especially from self-regulatory responses elaborated by private industry. The role of government is overturned from its classical conception as an entity that acts externally and outside of markets, although the GFC has provided evidence for the opposite conclusion, a counter-trend, with the re-emergence and reaffirmation of a new Westphalian system that aims to reframe and disempower the traditional role of independent agencies in financial regulation. Although other scholars[16] identify a new role for government as an entity that is external to the market, there are also other clear instances where government exercises a fundamental role that is internal to markets. For this reason, it can be just as misleading to illustrate the global governance of financial markets as a public-private divide as it is a potential misconception to theorise an insolvency law framework within the public-private divide with respect to failing financial institutions or collapsing private businesses (see Chapter 1). Today, macro-objectives follow micro-objectives and *vice versa*. Furthermore, beyond regulation's purposes that are getting closer, sometimes governments act in a "market actor role" using private means to public ends, and in so doing they behave as private actors in markets.[17]

---

16 Robert C. Hockett, Saule T. Omarova, "Private means to 'public' ends: Government as market actors" (2014) 1016 Cornell Law Faculty Publications 54, 55.

17 Ibid, 56. The authors first mention the existence of private laws that exercise a foundational role of the markets such as laws establishing proprietary interests in market exchange or contract law in the case of future performance in market exchange. Furthermore, they identify for expository purposes four different forms of the "market actor role" of governments, namely "market-making", "market-moving", "market-levering", and "market-preserving". Governments in "market-making" roles bear risks that private actors are "unable or unwilling to bear" such as the risk that

These new paradigms of global governance of financial markets have necessarily contributed to the emergence of the idea that what I term "macro-legislations" are progressively abandoned. A macro-legislation is an attempt to deal with almost every sector of the financial market (for instance, the Dodd-Frank Act in the United States). As opposed to macro-legislations, today, we experience the existence of "micro-legislations" at national level both to deal with an emerging new crisis such as Covid-19 in a temporary manner (the rise of national emergency measures) and to modify entire national legal frameworks in compliance with established best practices and standards agreed by private organisations (IMF, WBG, UNCITRAL, etc.) at the international level and determined by global legal indicators that serve the role of measuring the performance of national legal frameworks.

Indeed, today, in contemporary financial markets, the idea of top-down state regulation is not followed strictly, and the principle of exclusive sovereignty of the state has been diluted to the implementation of more dynamic sources of power reflected – at international level – in the frameworks of international financial organisations, rather than treaty-based regimes (such as the Basle Capital Accord of 1998, the Basle Core Principles for Effective Banking Supervision 1997, the Basle Concordat 1983, and the Code of Good Practices on Transparency in Monetary and Financial Policies Rules sponsored by the IMF). These acts are not international treaties and, therefore, cannot be defined as a classic source of public international law. However, they constitute part of the international financial architecture in which soft law plays an eminent role as a form of self-regulation. Essentially, in contemporary financial markets, the code of practices, or guidelines on corporate standards, or even a communication by the European Commission, is preferred and can play an essential role that is sometimes preferable to a static and written civil code. Nonetheless, there are still a few instances of treaty-based regulations, such as the General Agreement on Trade in Services or the North American Free Trade Agreement in North America. Finally, the regional agreements in Europe also play a vital role in the development of European financial regulation, such as the proposal for a capital markets union by the European Commission as well as the free movement of capital enshrined in the Treaty on the Functioning of the European Union. In all those instances, the main aim is the liberalisation of financial instruments rather than the imposition of regulation

---

some products will not be sold on the market, and they agree to act as a "buyer of last resort" through a private means that is underwriting. Governments in "market-moving" roles affect prices on certain markets instead of allowing private actors to do this, for instance, when central banks open market operations such as the purchasing or selling of treasury securities or "short-selling commodities whose quantitative easing-inflated prices disproportionately harm the poor". Governments in "market-levering" form can improve existing private markets' outcomes, such as in the case of public pensions whose investments can influence the practices of other firms, and finally, when they act in "market-preserving" roles possible collapses of the market are prevented in order to avoid negative externalities, in other words, it is the role of the government to act as a collective agent.

and the supervision of financial markets. It can be seen too that the role of public international law has changed from a classic conception of sources of international law.

4.4 Conclusions

Global legal indicators play a remarkable role in building the new financial architecture beyond structural crises. As we have seen, global legal indicators follow a rational managerial approach by measuring the performance of national legal frameworks in accordance with (legal) constants that are established and enshrined in quasi-legal frameworks, rather than hard law provisions. The Core Principles, the UNCITRAL Model Law on Cross-Border Insolvency, and the Principles for Effective Insolvency and Creditor/Debtor Regimes that we have illustrated in this chapter are just some of the new instances that are always more often established at the international level as legal parameters, or benchmarks against which national legislations are assessed. This shift in practice not only reflects a vision of managing risks under the laws of probabilities (Chapter 3) and through managerial rationality, but rather specifically promotes a re-evaluation of uncertainty as one of the driven forces of money creation processes under which new financing can be secured for preventing restructuring or as a means of investing in the private sectors of developing and emerging countries.

The role of well-designed insolvency frameworks in facilitating the extension of credit and private sector development is indeed widely recognised. In many cases, countries might choose to have several of these procedures within their legal framework in order to provide stakeholders with a variety of tools to address financial distress. Addressing the financial difficulties of a business at an early stage is critical for a successful turnaround and has been a recurrent trend since 2009. Often, these procedures restrict the direct involvement of the court and allocate a greater role to private negotiations between the debtor and its creditors. Nonetheless, reorganisation or restructuring frameworks can take many different forms and are adaptable to each country's financial and real sectors' specific needs. As each country develops their own restructuring tools and procedures suitable to address their needs and complement their current framework, it is sometimes difficult to classify them in specific typologies and sometimes the dividing line between the processes might not be so clear.

We have seen in Chapter 1 how insolvency law is subject to changing dynamics that can be drawn from the new elements introduced in the latest European reforms where we have witnessed a move towards new procedures that combine court intervention with private negotiations of the parties (the so-called "hybrid mechanisms"), which represents an evolution towards pre-packaged reorganisation and expedited restructurings in general. This new trend was strongly endorsed by the European Commission in March 2014 with its Recommendation on a new approach to business failure and insolvency and the Commission's proposal in November 2016 for a directive on preventive restructuring frameworks. Like the Principles for Effective Insolvency and Creditor Rights prepared by the World

Bank Group, the Restructuring Directive takes into consideration several best practices in preventive restructuring, aiming at expediting the rescue of companies, and it has taken inspiration from UK schemes of arrangement and, to an even greater extent, bankruptcy proceedings under Chapter 11 of the US Bankruptcy Code. The proposals are ambitious and far-reaching. Since then, a number of countries in Western Europe, including Italy, Germany, and Spain, have introduced new composition procedures for early restructuring of corporate debtors that are not yet technically insolvent, a trend that has been followed in the EBRD region in countries such as Croatia and Slovenia. Another mechanism that has become popular as a means of expediting the restructuring process is the "pre-pack", a reorganisation plan that is pre-agreed with a majority of creditors prior to submission to the court. Albania and Serbia have incorporated the "pre-pack" into their insolvency legislation.

Despite the many forms and possible restructuring tools that a country can incorporate, this chapter has hopefully outlined the new legislative process of years to come, namely a de-centralised legal system with a global governance that is informed by cooperation mechanisms and with the interaction of multiple private organisations at international level. This new apex contributes to the uncodified-codification process that we have explored throughout this work. Whereas benchmarks are established at the international level, the executive decisions of implementation through legislation or statute law are taken at national level, so that the original apex that was once personified by the national state with its sovereign power becomes the new periphery or "execution-centre". It is a new encounter of the global-local that is so distant from the times when the law was seen as a rebellious tool (the French and American Revolutions), and it encompasses the law as an "output" and an administrative instrument.

Conclusions

The Covid-19 pandemic is surely one of the greatest public health disasters the world has experienced in a century, although less deadly in comparison to the Black Death. This work has claimed that the economic fallout is very likely to exceed the GFC of 2007–2010. Although this time the trigger for the crisis was external rather than endemic to the financial system, the economic consequences cannot be overlooked, and are destined to pose new emerging challenges to future generations to come. Despite a pro-regulation approach that has long character-ised financial markets, at least since the inception of the GFC, with more attention to prudential requirements for banks, and a new role for financial regulation, this work has taken the stance that the role of law has dramatically changed since and even before the appearance of the Covid-19 pandemic in 2020. To this end, Covid-19 has merely been an accelerator of the changing process. Today, the law is the "output" rather than the "input" of every possible codification process and it is an administration tool to implement international law reforms.

Markets are full of risks. This should never worry us though, as risks can and should be understood as profitable opportunities, especially where we can miti-gate against them. But markets are also just as full of uncertainties; unknowns that cannot be quantified as risks, cannot be mitigated against, and which may offer heightened profit opportunities, but which can also spell disaster. Recalling Frank Knight's core 1921 message, this time around with application to financial markets, this work has offered a re-interpretation of risks, uncertainty, and profit, and it has highlighted the difficult role the law plays, or sometimes does not play, in regulating them.

The financial system depends on confidence. The system works because socie-ties have confidence in it and accept cheques in payment of debt. This is a purely social construct based on trust. For this reason, it could be said that the financial system is fragile. However, it is rare that currencies lose value and cease to func-tion. This usually happens only in wartime such as in Germany in the 1930s or when cryptocurrencies are adopted as a legal tender with the unique example of El Salvador in 2021. It is more common for financial institutions or individual banks to fail. The banking industry is particularly fragile because it depends on the confidence of depositors who must be assured the bank will repay their depos-its, despite the bank having lent these deposits out at longer terms to borrowers.

Furthermore, the financial system as a whole depends on different players, such as the provider of currency who must avoid issuing it too fast to prevent devaluation; the payment system that should be able to guarantee the delivery of payments to the intended recipients; savings that should be made available to users in order to sustain business activities, house purchases, and so on. For these reasons, society looks to central banks to prevent these inherent fragilities and mitigate their effects. Indeed, one of the main functions of central banks is to maintain a stable currency; that means avoiding extreme inflation or deflation. The necessarily unknowable feature of uncertainty can nevertheless constitute a hurdle for any form of supervision or regulation, so central banks or financial regulators must not be blamed. Uncertainty-aversion paradigms – as we mentioned in Chapter 3 – cannot be easily implemented, and in addition, they can reduce the ability to generate profit.

Nonetheless, in times of crisis, financial regulators can tackle economic bubbles by assessing the future in two ways: the ontological vision and the epistemological explanation. From an epistemological point of view, economic bubbles can occur, but we cannot predict when they happen, and we can only limit the damage caused by the bubble and try to prevent an economic crisis from happening. On the other hand, in the ontological view, economic bubbles do not exist and, therefore, damage limitation can occur only after a crisis has appeared. In both cases, regulatory disasters cannot be totally avoided. Indeed, in an epistemological conception, a financial regulator might be blamed for over-regulation, whereas according to an ontological view, it might be too late to act. Hence, in Chapter 3, we claimed a re-interpretation of uncertainty as a market structure, a feature of financial systems and a necessary element that cannot be avoided, prevented, or calculated in advance.

The global pandemic saw a lot of winners and losers in the world of business, including having an enormous effect on everyday life in universities across the globe. From Zoom seminars to locked-down halls, the education industry's figures are not dissimilar to those of today's business industries. Take the UK, for example, where the total income of the universities sector is around £40bn a year, half of which comes from tuition fees; overseas students account for around £7bn of this tuition fee income. Covid-19 is having a serious impact on the finances of the higher education system, including short-term lockdown-related costs and financial losses on long-term investments. In July 2020, the Institute for Fiscal Studies predicted that a decrease in overseas students due to Covid-19 could be responsible for a loss of up to £4bn. The outlook is similar in the United States, although Biden's $1.9tn American Rescue Plan has pledged $40bn to help support US higher education institutions through Covid-19, with a specific emphasis on those with an endowment under $1m. Uncertainties are once again dominating the scene at international level, and in the face of economic downturn and eroded capital reserves, both in private and public companies, insolvency could lead to debt restructuring, takeovers and mergers, or closure.

A modern and progressive insolvency law framework matters. We saw in Chapters 1 and 4 how insolvency law frameworks can help to save distressed businesses from a fatal destiny of liquidation. Today, the progressive role of insolvency practices is based on non-insolvency rules, or better, preventing restructuring. At the European level, we have examined the Restructuring Directive of 20 June 2019. All the 27 EU member states were obliged to implement the European Restructuring Directive by 17 July 2021. The directive was in part a reaction to the phenomenon of continental European companies in a financial crisis restructuring their debt under an English Scheme of Arrangement. The Scheme of Arrangement, which is not an insolvency process, offers the chance to implement debt restructuring on the basis of a majority decision by the creditors. This means that a single holdout creditor cannot block a reasonable restructuring plan if the majority of creditors approve it. Many European countries did not offer this valuable option outside of an insolvency. Indeed, insolvencies are value-destructive and lower the prospects of a recovery for creditors. The directive made it mandatory for EU member states to offer a preventive restructuring framework. Preventive restructuring is an evolved form of commercial law that focuses on hybrid restructuring mechanisms based on a mix of elements ranging from a minimal court-supervised approach to a consistent out-of-court feature based on private arrangement or workouts.

This new configuration of the law, which – as we said – is no longer based on a classic conception of insolvency, is leading to a transformation of legal meanings and constants outside of the law (see Chapters 2 and 4). Countries around the globe had started to understand the importance of preventing restructuring even before Covid-19, but the appearance of the pandemic – as we have said – has definitively accelerated the process of legal implementations. The modification of national laws is directed by international organisations rather than national parliaments. It is within this new role of international practices that national states seek cooperation and establish consolidated practices and principles to be followed as a guidance in the enactment of new laws. The work has specifically taken into account the importance of this new cooperation at international level in the field of insolvency law frameworks that offers a way of testing the theory of (legal) constant(s). The EBRD's Core Principles, the World Bank's Principles for Effective Insolvency and Creditor/Debtor Regimes, and the UNCITRAL Legislative Guide to Insolvency Law represent the most vivid examples of this new "codification" of the law, or better, of the new uncodified-codification of the law. Unlike in the past, this new codification process starts from out-of-law principles that are then transposed and transformed into hard law provisions of national legal frameworks. The establishment of specific insolvency law principles is the direct outcome of the continuous discussions that are encouraged and promoted by international institutions such as IMF and INSOL International. In other words, the principles correspond to the practical needs and hurdles that are experienced and reported by national practitioners in domestic jurisdictions. Furthermore, the WBG as well as the EBRD and other international organisations have developed over time specific indicators to measure the effectiveness of insolvency law frameworks. The principles settled at international level thus reflect the best practices in the sector that they are aiming to assess, in this case, insolvency law.

A modernised insolvency law framework attracts a higher level of capital and investments. At no time has competition mattered so much, and financial innovation and creativity are essential to keep businesses alive and on the market.[1] This shift is also particularly evident in traditional industries such as car dealerships, now looking for a new business model, as the way people buy and sell cars is changing. More customers are comfortable with completing transactions remotely. This shift actually started before the pandemic but accelerated as Covid-19 spurred people to do more of their shopping from home and demand for cars unexpectedly surged. Other parts of the business world have also been upended by e-commerce. National chains, rather than local small businesses, will set prices and give salespeople less room to haggle. Dealers will hold fewer cars on the lot and operate more like service-and-delivery centres.

While sometimes the pandemic has accelerated the adoption of new business models, at other times, it has simply provided the right ground for already existent business models. For instance, one industry that certainly benefitted from the effects of a global shutdown was home food delivery. When Deliveroo in the UK announced its IPO on the UK stock market in March 2021, the company could not have wished for better conditions. After a year of almost constant lockdowns, the experience of eating out that so many missed turned people to Deliveroo in their droves, causing the biggest upsurge in takeaway demand the industry had ever seen. An even wider change is taking place in the world of investing and financing. The term ESG stands for environmental, social, and corporate governance, referring to the three main factors considered when assessing a company's potential for sustainable investment in the long term and with it, its likelihood of turning a profit. Ethical investing is gaining in popularity, ESG funds are today offered by investment companies such as BlackRock, Aviva, and so on offering the ability to invest while avoiding ethically "questionable" areas such as big oil or arms trading. We might qualify such changing investment aptitude as "moral" investing. Whatever you name it, despite our efforts to change our own attitude towards investing or producing, no one can control, anticipate, or modify the consequences deriving from uncertainty, although it is in our own abilities to influence the final outcomes. In Chapter 3, a deep analysis from an epistemological point of view concluded that the knowledge of uncertainty is the knowledge of the impossible. This means that whatever label we invent to better qualify our actions, the final results will still be determined by the transformative features of uncertainty. To this end, a "green future" is equivalent to an uncertain future full of anxieties, no matter how you call it. Definitions are obsolete and part of a superseded past, although they are a remarkable sign of revolutions and changing factors. In fact, definitions were important in the codification era of the birth of the new modern state which, following the French Revolution, the absence of the monarch, and the increased role of the parliament brought lawmakers to enact

---

1 We have seen how contemporary financial markets are determined by four different structures: risk, uncertainty, competition, and financial innovation.

civil codes with a view to codifying any possible human or natural behaviour that could determine a legal effect. This approach was then intensified and further theorised with Hans Kelsen, who expressly separated the moral and religious sphere from the legal space. Nonetheless, Kelsen in his imagination of the ideal constitution of the state speaks of an uncodified legal provision that is not generated by the legal system, but at the same time, it provides that system with legal enforceability and legitimacy: the *grundnorm*. Kelsen does not give the reader a particular reasoning on whether the *grundnorm* is created by a legal provision or it is pre-ordered to the legal system. One way to justify its existence, but at the same time to contravene the entire legal theory of Kelsen, which is fundamentally based on the conception of the law as "input", is to perceive the *grundnorm* as a fact, hence outside of the law. I find Kelsen particularly engaging for our discussion of (legal) constants where we have claimed that the law is an "output". This further evolution can help us interpret the new financial architecture we live in today.

The secularisation of the state, and the separation of moral principles from legal arguments, is at the core of the old world, the world of Kelsen where codifications matter. The world of Pistor is one where private and public interests are rendered legal and vindicated by virtue of codification processes. Today, as this work has claimed, the new financial architecture of contemporary financial markets – or better, financial systems – is expressly based on sustainability and it is decided at the "periphery" rather than at the apex due to the absence of a central planner or supreme architect of the financial system. Sustainability is a (legal) constant. It is a non-legal term that has become legal by virtue of quasi-legal frameworks such as policy statements, guidelines, and generally, soft law instruments that are non-binding and non-enforceable. Nonetheless, we have seen how this non-enforceability can still create a modification of the legal environment due to the spontaneous compliance and auto-imposed self-regulation practices of market operators.

Furthermore, sustainability pays. Investors are turning away from old models of exploiting natural resources and workers who produce them, though there is also significant money to be made by doing so. Some funds aim to help investors take an "avoid" strategy, which seeks to remove from a portfolio certain companies or industries that are associated with a higher ESG risk profile. Another alternative option is to use an "advance" strategy: rather than working by process of elimination, this strategy instead seeks to specifically pursue or prioritise companies or sectors that are viewed as sustainable, progressive, and having a positive ESG profile, such as "green" energy. There is an increased demand for ethical investing coupled with easier access to investing in the stock market; with apps like Robinhood, Mint, or eToro, more and more ESG-focused products are coming to market, and in some cases, the uptake for these is greater than with traditional exchange traded funds or index tracker funds.

Another effect of Covid-19 has been the chance to slow down and consider how we spend our money. The closing of shops and the slowing of industry was a unique opportunity to take stock and reflect on the relentless spending culture we live in, and the attendant environmental and social concerns that this raises.

Covid-19 has had a massive impact on our lives, but not necessarily for the worse; in recovering from the coronavirus and in securing an environmentally sustainable and profitable future, companies will need to adapt or suffer the consequences, whether that be for their social and human rights practices or simple reputation. For example, Deliveroo is not the only business that has been hit with a raft of accusations of shady working practices, poor treatment of workers, and taking advantage of the very individuals whose technical skills, networks, ingenuity, and plain old hard work helped them build big capital in the first place. Energy companies may shout about investing in renewables, but until we experience a global shift away from their reliance on fossil fuels, accusations would appear to be justified.

It is undeniable that Covid-19 has represented a major threat to national economies, but at the same time, it has been a unique change factor for business models. It is likely – as we said in Chapter 3 – that the current pandemic may one day become endemic, and destined to stay around, especially due to the many variants that can be generated over time. Whereas we can control or mitigate infection risk through masking and vaccines, we cannot anticipate or control variants. Those are the product of uncertainty. In times of crisis, the fallout exposes weaknesses in national economies and international supply chains. Consequently, it may be the case that we will witness a retreat from globalisation, or better, new ways to live in a globalised world. Indeed, if risk-taking is the main form of progress, we shall and we must continue to evolve towards this pattern because any uncertainty-aversion paradigm necessarily leads to profit-destruction outcomes. Uncertainty underpins rather than undermines profit. In times of crisis, no matter what the trigger may be or where the next shock may come from, whether you take an ontological or epistemological view on economic bubbles, what matters is the ability of a country to build consistent and harmonious relationships between financial law and international insolvency, or cross-border insolvency. In light of this, we can also assert that international insolvency and financial law are, indeed, constants in times of crisis. This is because the emergence of significant non-financial enterprises is a compelling reality that requires answers and ways to prevent the disruptive effects of their possible collapse. The new financial architecture is based on sustainability. Sustainability becomes a (legal) constant rich in meanings that become relevant for financial law, insolvency law, sovereign debt relief practices, corporate governance, and environmental law in an out-of-law search for non-legal meanings that from now on seem difficult to end. The codification era has just ended and the instauration or initiation of the future of (legal) constants and out-of-law meanings has just started.

Index

Note: 'n' after a page reference indicates the number of a note on that page.

American Revolution 48, 78
Argentina 12, 22

Bank Recovery and Resolution Directive
    (BRRD) 28
Bernoulli, David 54, 58
Bernstein, Peter L. 51n4
Bitcoin 8, 14–15
Black Death 51, 79
borrowers 15–16, 19–20, 22, 51, 57–58,
    65–66, 79

Cardano, Girolamo 51
central banks 2, 4, 17, 17n24, 23,
    76n17, 80
central planner 6, 12, 21, 29, 34, 44, 48,
    58, 60–61, 74, 83
China 27–29, 31, 52
Chinese Estates Holding (CEH) 27
Code of Capital 13, 34–35, 40, 47, 65, 74
codification 5, 13–14, 23, 26, 34–36,
    40–41, 46–48, 61, 63–65, 74, 78–79,
    81–84
collective action clause (CAC) 10n3,
    12–13
Common Frame of Reference (CFR) 45
competition 7, 19, 36–37, 39, 49, 56–61,
    69, 75, 82, 82n1
Convention on Contracts for the
    International Sale of Goods (CISG) 45
Core Principles of Insolvency (Core
    Principles) 63, 72–73, 76–77, 81
corporate social responsibility (CSR) 68
Covid-19 1–5, 14, 21–23, 25, 27, 33, 41,
    47, 52–53, 55, 58, 63, 70, 72, 74, 76,
    79–84; Delta variant 52–53; Omicron
    variant 53

D'Alvia, Daniele 14n12, 19n39, 45n7,
    51n2, 55n11
debt service suspension initiative
    (DSSI) 22
Deliveroo 82, 84
diversity 8, 23, 36

environment 5, 8, 12, 16, 24, 36–37, 47,
    55–60, 62, 74, 83
environmental, social, and corporate
    governance (ESG) 5, 23, 82–83
European Bank for Reconstruction and
    Development (EBRD) 6, 63, 72–73,
    78, 81
European Commission (EC) 24, 25n57,
    43n5, 76–77
European Union (EU) 2–3, 16, 16n20,
    24–25, 39–40, 44–45, 48, 70, 73, 76, 81
Evergrande 27

Federal Reserve 1, 1n2, 2n3, 4
Federal Reserve System (Fed) 2, 2n2
Fermat, Pierre 51
Fibonacci, Leonardo 51
financial: architecture 6, 22–23, 36, 49,
    73, 76–77, 83–84; assets 9–10, 14,
    20–21, 20n42; crises 3, 7, 10, 14, 17n26,
    18–19, 30, 36, 41, 47, 50, 56–57, 59,
    64, 73, 81; difficulties 26, 31–33, 35,
    64, 69–70, 72–73, 77; innovation 7,
    13, 19, 20n42, 36–37, 49, 56–61, 82,
    82n1; instruments 9–10, 13, 76; law 84;
    markets 1–3, 5–9, 13, 15–21, 17n28, 31,
    36–37, 49–51, 53, 55–61, 55n11, 74–77,
    79, 82n1, 83; operations 9, 18, 36, 74;
    regulation 3, 15, 17n27, 20, 59, 74–76,
    79–80; risk 15, 19, 49–50, 58–59, 61,

68, 74–75; stability 4, 17, 17n24, 26, 28, 72; system 3–4, 7, 9, 19, 24, 37, 55–61, 55n11, 63, 74, 79–80, 83; technology (Fintech) 36, 39
French Revolution 7, 48, 78, 82

Galileo 51
Georgieva, Kristalina 2, 21n45
Giddens, Anthony 51, 51n3
Global Financial Crisis (GFC) 3–4, 14–15, 17, 24, 50, 58, 67, 72–73, 75, 79
global legal indicators 63, 67–69, 76–77
Graunt, John 51
Green, David 17n23
gross domestic product (GDP) 2, 4

Halley, Edmond 51
Hong Kong 27–29

initial public offering (IPO) 1, 26, 82
insolvency: bank 17n28, 26–27; corporate 5–6, 24, 26, 64; cross-border 26, 28, 34, 61, 70–71, 73, 77, 84; law assessments (ILAs) 6, 37, 61, 72–73; *see also* law
Insolvency Creditor Rights Standard (ICR Standard) 63
International Association of Restructuring, Insolvency and Bankruptcy Professionals (INSOL) 24, 24n53, 81
International Capital Market Association (ICMA) 12–13, 12n9, 36, 48
International Institute for the Unification of Private Law (UNIDROIT) 11, 45
International Monetary Fund (IMF) 2, 10n3, 21–22, 22n50, 23n51, 34, 34n71, 36, 48, 63, 74, 76, 81
International Swaps and Derivative Association (ISDA) 6, 12–13, 36, 48

Kelsen, Hans 41, 60, 60n17, 83
Keynes, John Maynard 20
Knight, Frank 19, 54, 58–59, 79
Kötz, Hein 38, 38n1

Ladeur, Heinz 60, 60n15
Lastra, Rosa Maria 16n22, 17n28, 18n33
law: common 41, 42n5, 46, 66–67; contract 9, 32, 36, 42n5, 44–45, 64–66, 75n17; hard 5–6, 8, 12, 28, 36–37, 44–45, 47, 61, 63, 74, 77, 81; insolvency 5–6, 14, 21, 24, 26, 28–29, 31, 33–34, 37, 39, 44, 47, 61, 63–65, 67, 69–73, 75, 77, 80–82, 84; soft 6–7, 11–12, 14, 21,

28, 36–37, 45, 47, 61, 63, 74, 76, 83; statute 14, 46, 64, 78; *see also* financial
legal: indicators 67–69; institutions 38–43, 69; reforms 64, 68; systems 12, 14–15, 32, 35, 38, 40–43, 42n5, 46–47, 68, 72
legal theory of finance (LTF) 9, 13, 35, 59
Legal Transition Programme (LTP) 72
legislation: macro- 74, 76; micro- 74, 76
Legislative Guide on Insolvency Law 63, 69–72
Lehman Brothers 16, 24, 50, 58
Lender of Last Resort (LOLR) 17
lenders 15, 19–20, 51, 65–67
liquidity 2–3, 9–10, 17, 19, 27, 36
Luhmann, Niklas 7, 19, 19n41, 55–57, 55n11, 61–62

Milton, John 50
Moderna 52

network 1, 8, 36, 43n5, 56, 60, 69, 84
Noam, Eli M. 60, 60n16

Olivares-Caminal, Rodrigo 15n13, 17n28, 23n52

pandemic 2–4, 14, 21–23, 25, 27, 30, 34–36, 40, 47, 50, 52–53, 70, 79–82, 84; *see also* Black Death; Covid-19
pari passu 12, 36, 64–67
Pascal, Blaise 51
payment 10, 15–16, 18n37, 27, 32, 36, 39, 42n5, 43, 43n5, 47, 65–66, 74, 79–80
Pfizer 52
Pistor, Katharina 2, 5, 9–10, 9n1, 12–15, 13n11, 19, 23, 26, 34–36, 39, 41, 47, 65, 74, 83
Powell, Jerome 4
Principles of European Contract Law (PECL) 45
Principles of International Commercial Contracts (UPICC) 45
private: debt 3–4, 18, 26; sector 5, 72, 77; workout 21, 30–34, 39, 44

Recast Insolvency Regulation 24, 28
rescue 5–6, 21, 26–27, 30–36, 40, 44, 48, 64, 72–73, 78
Restructuring Directive 25–26, 34–36, 39, 44, 48, 61, 73, 78, 81
risk: contagion 52–53; high- 15–16, 15n16, 23, 65; measuring 51–52, 68; systemic 3–4, 17–19, 18n37, 26–27, 50;

-takers 19, 50–51, 54–55, 58–59, 61, 84;
see also financial

Sacco, Rodolfo 14, 38–39, 38n2, 41,
46–47
Siems, Mathias 67, 67n5
significant non-financial enterprise (SNFE)
26–27, 84
small-medium enterprise (SME) 71
Smith, Adam 75
special purpose vehicle (SPV) 66
Stablecoin 8
sustainability 5–6, 8, 22–23, 25, 35–36,
40, 83–84

Taylor, Frederick 68, 69n10

uncertainty 2–3, 5, 7, 9–10, 19–20, 36–37,
49–61, 74, 77, 79–80, 82, 82n1, 84
United Nations (UN) 7, 22, 69

United Nations Commission
on International Trade Law
(UNCITRAL) 11, 28, 28n64, 61,
63, 69–74, 76–77, 81
United States (US) 1, 3–4, 11, 15, 18n34,
25, 33, 48, 52, 57, 76, 78, 80

Vague, Richard 4, 4n7

Watson, Alan 14, 38, 38n3
World Bank 22, 22n48, 63, 71, 72n15, 81;
Group (WBG) 21, 21n47, 36, 48, 71,
73–74, 76, 81
World Bank Principles for Effective
Insolvency and Creditor/Debtor
Regimes (Principles) 63, 71–73, 77, 81

Yan, Hui Ka 27

Zweigert, Konrad 38, 38n1